FOREWORD

The collection of "Everything Will Be Okay" travel phrasebooks published by T&P Books is designed for people traveling abroad for tourism and business. The phrasebooks contain what matters most - the essentials for basic communication. This is an indispensable set of phrases to "survive" while abroad.

This phrasebook will help you in most cases where you need to ask something, get directions, find out how much something costs, etc. It can also resolve difficult communication situations where gestures just won't help.

This book contains a lot of phrases that have been grouped according to the most relevant topics. The edition also includes a small vocabulary that contains roughly 3,000 of the most frequently used words. Another section of the phrasebook provides a gastronomical dictionary that may help you order food at a restaurant or buy groceries at the store.

Take "Everything Will Be Okay" phrasebook with you on the road and you'll have an irreplaceable traveling companion who will help you find your way out of any situation and teach you to not fear speaking with foreigners.

TABLE OF CONTENTS

T&P Books Publishing

T&P Books Publishing

PHRASEBOOK
- BULGARIAN -

By Andrey Taranov

THE MOST IMPORTANT PHRASES

This phrasebook contains the most important phrases and questions for basic communication
Everything you need to survive overseas

T&P BOOKS

Phrasebook + 3000-word dictionary

English-Bulgarian phrasebook & topical vocabulary

By Andrey Taranov

The collection of "Everything Will Be Okay" travel phrasebooks published by T&P Books is designed for people traveling abroad for tourism and business. The phrasebooks contain what matters most - the essentials for basic communication. This is an indispensable set of phrases to "survive" while abroad.

This book also includes a small topical vocabulary that contains roughly 3,000 of the most frequently used words. Another section of the phrasebook provides a gastronomical dictionary that may help you order food at a restaurant or buy groceries at the store.

T&P Books Publishing
www.tpbooks.com

ISBN: 978-1-78492-455-3

This book is also available in E-book formats.
Please visit www.tpbooks.com or the major online bookstores.

PRONUNCIATION

T&P phonetic alphabet	Bulgarian example	English example
[a]	сладък [sládək]	shorter than in ask
[e]	череша [tʃeréʃa]	elm, medal
[i]	килим [kilím]	shorter than in feet
[o]	отломка [otlómka]	pod, John
[u]	улуча [ulútʃa]	book
[ə]	въже [vəʒé]	Schwa, rediced 'e'
[ja], [ʲa]	вечеря [vetʃérʲa]	royal
[ʲu]	ключ [klʲutʃ]	cued, cute
[ʲo]	фризьор [frizʲór]	New York
[ja], [ʲa]	история [istórija]	royal
[b]	събота [sébota]	baby, book
[d]	пладне [pládne]	day, doctor
[f]	парфюм [parfʲúm]	face, food
[g]	гараж [garáʒ]	game, gold
[ʒ]	мрежа [mréʒa]	forge, pleasure
[j]	двубой [dvubój]	yes, New York
[h]	храбър [hrábər]	huge, hat
[k]	колело [koleló]	clock, kiss
[l]	паралел [paralél]	lace, people
[m]	мяукам [mʲaúkam]	magic, milk
[n]	фонтан [fontán]	name, normal
[p]	пушек [púʃek]	pencil, private
[r]	крепост [krépost]	rice, radio
[s]	каса [kása]	city, boss
[t]	тютюн [tʲutʲún]	tourist, trip
[v]	завивам [zavívam]	very, river
[ts]	църква [tsérkva]	cats, tsetse fly
[ʃ]	шапка [ʃápka]	machine, shark
[tʃ]	чорапи [tʃorápi]	church, French
[w]	уиски [wíski]	vase, winter
[z]	зарзават [zarzavát]	zebra, please

5

LIST OF ABBREVIATIONS

English abbreviations

ab.	-	about
adj	-	adjective
adv	-	adverb
anim.	-	animate
as adj	-	attributive noun used as adjective
e.g.	-	for example
etc.	-	et cetera
fam.	-	familiar
fem.	-	feminine
form.	-	formal
inanim.	-	inanimate
masc.	-	masculine
math	-	mathematics
mil.	-	military
n	-	noun
pl	-	plural
pron.	-	pronoun
sb	-	somebody
sing.	-	singular
sth	-	something
v aux	-	auxiliary verb
vi	-	intransitive verb
vi, vt	-	intransitive, transitive verb
vt	-	transitive verb

Bulgarian abbreviations

ж	-	feminine noun
ж мн	-	feminine plural
м	-	masculine noun
м мн	-	masculine plural
м, ж	-	masculine, feminine
мн	-	plural
с	-	neuter
с мн	-	neuter plural

T&P BOOKS

BULGARIAN PHRASEBOOK

This section contains
important phrases that may
come in handy in various
real-life situations.
The phrasebook will help
you ask for directions, clarify
a price, buy tickets, and
order food at a restaurant

T&P Books Publishing

PHRASEBOOK
CONTENTS

T&P Books Publishing

The bare minimum

Excuse me, ...	**Извинете, ...** [izvinéte, ...]
Hello.	**Здравейте.** [zdravéjte]
Thank you.	**Благодаря.** [blagodarʲá]
Good bye.	**Довиждане.** [dovíʒdane]
Yes.	**Да.** [da]
No.	**Не.** [ne]
I don't know.	**Аз не знам.** [az ne znam]
Where? | Where to? | When?	**Къде? | Накъде? | Кога?** [kədé? | nakədé? | kogá?]

I need ...	**Трябва ми ...** [trʲábva mi ...]
I want ...	**Аз искам ...** [az ískam ...]
Do you have ...?	**Имате ли ...?** [ímate li ...?]
Is there a ... here?	**Тук има ли ...?** [tuk íma li ...?]
May I ...?	**Мога ли ...?** [móga li ...?]
..., please (polite request)	**Моля.** [mólʲa]

I'm looking for ...	**Аз търся ...** [az térsʲa ...]
the restroom	**тоалетна** [toalétna]
an ATM	**банкомат** [bankomát]
a pharmacy (drugstore)	**аптека** [aptéka]
a hospital	**болница** [bólnitsa]
the police station	**полицейски участък** [politséjski uʧástək]
the subway	**метро** [metró]

a taxi	**такси** [táksi]
the train station	**гара** [gára]

My name is …	**Казвам се …** [kázvam se …]
What's your name?	**Как се казвате?** [kak se kázvate?]
Could you please help me?	**Помогнете ми, моля.** [pomognéte mi, mólʲa]
I've got a problem.	**Аз имам проблем.** [az ímam problém]
I don't feel well.	**Лошо ми е.** [lóʃo mi e]
Call an ambulance!	**Повикайте бърза помощ!** [povikájte bérza pómoʃt!]
May I make a call?	**Може ли да се обадя?** [móʒe li da se obádʲa?]

I'm sorry.	**Извинявам се.** [izvinʲávam se]
You're welcome.	**Моля.** [mólʲa]

I, me	**аз** [az]
you (inform.)	**ти** [ti]
he	**той** [toj]
she	**тя** [tʲa]
they (masc.)	**те** [te]
they (fem.)	**те** [te]
we	**ние** [nie]
you (pl)	**вие** [víe]
you (sg, form.)	**Вие** [víe]

ENTRANCE	**ВХОД** [vhod]
EXIT	**ИЗХОД** [íshot]
OUT OF ORDER	**НЕ РАБОТИ** [ne ráboti]
CLOSED	**ЗАТВОРЕНО** [zatvóreno]

OPEN	**ОТВОРЕНО** [otvóreno]
FOR WOMEN	**ЗА ЖЕНИ** [za ʒení]
FOR MEN	**ЗА МЪЖЕ** [za məʒé]

Questions

Where?	**Къде?** [kədé?]
Where to?	**Накъде?** [nakədé?]
Where from?	**Откъде?** [otkədé?]
Why?	**Защо?** [zaʃtó?]
For what reason?	**По каква причина?** [po kakvá pritʃína?]
When?	**Кога?** [kogá?]

How long?	**За колко?** [za kólko?]
At what time?	**В колко?** [v kólko?]
How much?	**Колко струва?** [kólko strúva?]
Do you have ...?	**Имате ли ...?** [ímate li ...?]
Where is ...?	**Къде се намира ...?** [kədé se namíra ...?]

What time is it?	**Колко е часът?** [kólko e ʧasét?]
May I make a call?	**Може ли да се обадя?** [moʒe li da se obádia?]
Who's there?	**Кой е там?** [koj e tam?]
Can I smoke here?	**Мога ли тук да пуша?** [móga li tuk da púʃa?]
May I ...?	**Мога ли ...?** [móga li ...?]

Needs

I'd like …	**Аз бих искал /искала/ …** [az bih ískal /ískala/ …]
I don't want …	**Аз не искам …** [az ne ískam …]
I'm thirsty.	**Аз искам да пия.** [az ískam da pijá]
I want to sleep.	**Аз искам да спя.** [az ískam da spʲa]
I want …	**Аз искам …** [az ískam …]
to wash up	**да се измия** [da se izmijá]
to brush my teeth	**да си мия зъбите** [da si míja zəbíte]
to rest a while	**малко да си почина** [málko da si potʃína]
to change my clothes	**да се преоблека** [da se preobleká]
to go back to the hotel	**да се върна в хотела** [da se vérna v hotéla]
to buy …	**да купя …** [da kúpʲa …]
to go to …	**да отида …** [da otída …]
to visit …	**да посетя …** [da posetʲá …]
to meet with …	**да се срещна с …** [da se sréʃtna s …]
to make a call	**да се обадя** [da se obádʲa]
I'm tired.	**Аз се изморих.** [az se izmoríh]
We are tired.	**Ние се изморихме.** [nie se izmoríhme]
I'm cold.	**Студено ми е.** [studéno mi e]
I'm hot.	**Топло ми е.** [tóplo mi e]
I'm OK.	**Нормално ми е.** [normálno mi e]

I need to make a call.	**Трябва да се обадя.** [tr'ábva da se obád'a]
I need to go to the restroom.	**Искам да отида в тоалетната.** [ískam da otída v toalétnata]
I have to go.	**Трябва да тръгвам.** [tr'ábva da trégvam]
I have to go now.	**Сега трябва да тръгвам.** [segá tr'ábva da trégvam]

Asking for directions

Excuse me, ...	**Извинете, ...** [izvinéte, ...]
Where is ...?	**Къде се намира ...?** [kədé se namíra ...?]
Which way is ...?	**В коя посока се намира ...?** [v koja posóka se namíra ...?]
Could you help me, please?	**Помогнете ми, моля.** [pomognéte mi, mólʲa]

I'm looking for ...	**Аз търся ...** [az tərsʲa ...]
I'm looking for the exit.	**Аз търся изход.** [az tərsʲa íshot]
I'm going to ...	**Аз пътувам до ...** [az pətúvam do ...]
Am I going the right way to ...?	**Правилно ли вървя ...?** [právilno li vərvʲá ...?]

Is it far?	**Далече ли е?** [dalétʃe li e?]
Can I get there on foot?	**Ще стигна ли дотам пеша?** [ʃte stígna li dotám péʃa?]
Can you show me on the map?	**Покажете ми на картата, моля.** [pokaʒéte mi na kártata, mólʲa]
Show me where we are right now.	**Покажете, къде сме сега.** [pokaʒéte, kədé sme segá]

Here	**Тук** [tuk]
There	**Там** [tam]
This way	**Тука** [túka]

Turn right.	**Завийте надясно.** [zavíjte nadʲásno]
Turn left.	**Завийте наляво.** [zavíjte nalʲávo]
first (second, third) turn	**първи (втори, трети) завой** [pərvi (ftóri, tréti) zavój]
to the right	**надясно** [nadʲásno]

to the left

наляво
[naľávo]

Go straight ahead.

Вървете направо.
[vərvéte naprávo]

Signs

WELCOME!	**ДОБРЕ ДОШЛИ!** [dobré doʃlí!]
ENTRANCE	**ВХОД** [vhod]
EXIT	**ИЗХОД** [íshot]
PUSH	**БУТНИ** [butní]
PULL	**ДРЪПНИ** [drəpní]
OPEN	**ОТВОРЕНО** [otvóreno]
CLOSED	**ЗАТВОРЕНО** [zatvóreno]
FOR WOMEN	**ЗА ЖЕНИ** [za ʒení]
FOR MEN	**ЗА МЪЖЕ** [za məʒé]
GENTLEMEN, GENTS	**МЪЖКА ТОАЛЕТНА** [méʒka toalétna]
WOMEN	**ЖЕНСКА ТОАЛЕТНА** [ʒénska toalétna]
DISCOUNTS	**НАМАЛЕНИЯ** [namalénija]
SALE	**РАЗПРОДАЖБА** [rasprodáʒba]
FREE	**БЕЗПЛАТНО** [besplátno]
NEW!	**НОВИНА!** [noviná!]
ATTENTION!	**ВНИМАНИЕ!** [vnimánie!]
NO VACANCIES	**НЯМА МЕСТА** [nʲáma mestá]
RESERVED	**РЕЗЕРВИРАНО** [rezervírano]
ADMINISTRATION	**АДМИНИСТРАЦИЯ** [administrátsija]
STAFF ONLY	**САМО ЗА ПЕРСОНАЛА** [sámo za personála]

BEWARE OF THE DOG!	**ЛОШО КУЧЕ** [lóʃo kutʃe]
NO SMOKING!	**НЕ СЕ ПУШИ!** [ne se púʃi!]
DO NOT TOUCH!	**НЕ ПИПАЙ С РЪЦЕТЕ!** [ne pipáj s rətséte!]
DANGEROUS	**ОПАСНО** [opásno]
DANGER	**ОПАСНОСТ** [opásnost]
HIGH VOLTAGE	**ВИСОКО НАПРЕЖЕНИЕ** [visóko napreʒénie]
NO SWIMMING!	**КЪПАНЕТО Е ЗАБРАНЕНО** [képaneto e zabranéno]
OUT OF ORDER	**НЕ РАБОТИ** [ne ráboti]
FLAMMABLE	**ОГНЕОПАСНО** [ogneopásno]
FORBIDDEN	**ЗАБРАНЕНО** [zabranéno]
NO TRESPASSING!	**ПРЕМИНАВАНЕТО Е ЗАБРАНЕНО** [preminávaneto e zabranéno]
WET PAINT	**БОЯДИСАНО** [bojadísano]
CLOSED FOR RENOVATIONS	**ЗАТВОРЕНО ЗА РЕМОНТ** [zatvóreno za remónt]
WORKS AHEAD	**РЕМОНТНИ РАБОТИ** [remóntni ráboti]
DETOUR	**ЗАОБИКАЛЯНЕ** [zaobikálʲane]

Transportation. General phrases

plane	**самолет** [samolét]
train	**влак** [vlak]
bus	**автобус** [aftobús]
ferry	**ферибот** [féribot]
taxi	**такси** [táksi]
car	**кола** [kóla]
schedule	**разписание** [raspisánie]
Where can I see the schedule?	**Къде мога да видя разписанието?** [kədé móga da vídʲa raspisánieto?]
workdays (weekdays)	**работни дни** [rabótni dni]
weekends	**почивни дни** [potʃívni dni]
holidays	**празнични дни** [práznitʃni dni]
DEPARTURE	**ЗАМИНАВАНЕ** [zaminávane]
ARRIVAL	**ПРИСТИГАНЕ** [pristígane]
DELAYED	**ЗАКЪСНЯВА** [zakəsnʲáva]
CANCELLED	**ОТМЕНЕН** [otmenén]
next (train, etc.)	**следващ** [slédvaʃt]
first	**първи** [pérvi]
last	**последен** [posléden]
When is the next ...?	**Кога е следващият ...?** [kogá e slédvaʃtijat ...?]
When is the first ...?	**Кога тръгва първият ...?** [kogá trégva pérvijat ...?]

When is the last …?

Кога тръгва последният …?
[kogá trégva póslednijat …?]

transfer (change of trains, etc.)

прекачване
[prekátʃvane]

to make a transfer

да правя прекачване
[da právʲa prekátʃvane]

Do I need to make a transfer?

Трябва ли да правя прекачване?
[trʲábva li da právʲa prekátʃvane?]

Buying tickets

Where can I buy tickets?	**Къде мога да купя билети?** [kədé móga da kúp'a biléti?]
ticket	**билет** [bilét]
to buy a ticket	**да купя билет** [da kúp'a bilét]
ticket price	**цена на билета** [tsená na biléta]
Where to?	**Накъде?** [nakədé?]
To what station?	**До коя станция?** [do kojá stántsija?]
I need ...	**Трябва ми ...** [tr'ábva mi ...]
one ticket	**един билет** [edín bilét]
two tickets	**два билета** [dva biléta]
three tickets	**три билета** [tri biléta]
one-way	**в една посока** [v edná posóka]
round-trip	**отиване и връщане** [otívane i vrɛ́ʃtane]
first class	**първа класа** [pɛ́rva klása]
second class	**втора класа** [ftóra klása]
today	**днес** [dnes]
tomorrow	**утре** [útre]
the day after tomorrow	**вдругиден** [vdrúgiden]
in the morning	**сутринта** [sutrínta]
in the afternoon	**през деня** [prez den'á]
in the evening	**вечерта** [vetʃertá]

aisle seat	**място до коридора** [mʲásto do koridóra]
window seat	**място до прозореца** [mʲásto do prozóretsa]
How much?	**Колко?** [kólko?]
Can I pay by credit card?	**Мога ли да платя с карта?** [móga li da platʲá s kárta?]

Bus

bus	**автобус** [aftobús]
intercity bus	**междуградски автобус** [meʒdugrátski aftobús]
bus stop	**автобусна спирка** [aftobúsna spírka]
Where's the nearest bus stop?	**Къде се намира най-близката автобусна спирка?** [kədé se namíra naj-blízkata aftobúsna spírka?]

number (bus ~, etc.)	**номер** [nómer]
Which bus do I take to get to ...?	**Кой номер автобус отива до ...?** [koj nómer aftobús otíva do ...?]
Does this bus go to ...?	**Този автобус отива ли до ...?** [tózi aftobús otíva li do ...?]
How frequent are the buses?	**Кога има автобуси?** [kogá íma aftobúsi?]

every 15 minutes	**на всеки 15 минути** [na fséki petnádeset minúti]
every half hour	**на всеки половин час** [na fséki polovín ʧas]
every hour	**на всеки час** [na fséki ʧas]
several times a day	**няколко пъти на ден** [nʲákolko péti na den]
... times a day	**... пъти на ден** [... péti na den]

schedule	**разписание** [raspisánie]
Where can I see the schedule?	**Къде мога да видя разписанието?** [kədé móga da vídʲa raspisánieto?]
When is the next bus?	**Кога е следващият автобус?** [kogá e slédvaʃtijat aftobús?]
When is the first bus?	**Кога тръгва първият автобус?** [kogá trəgva pérvijat aftobús?]
When is the last bus?	**Кога заминава последният автобус?** [kogá zamináva slédnijat aftobús?]

stop	**спирка** [spírka]
next stop	**следваща спирка** [slédvaʃta spírka]
last stop (terminus)	**последна спирка** [poslédna spírka]
Stop here, please.	**Спрете тук, моля.** [spréte tuk, mólʲa]
Excuse me, this is my stop.	**Може ли, това е моята спирка.** [móʒe li, tová e mójata spírka]

Train

train	**влак** [vlak]
suburban train	**крайградски влак** [krajgrátski vlak]
long-distance train	**влак за далечни разстояния** [vlak za dalétʃni rasstojánija]
train station	**гара** [gára]
Excuse me, where is the exit to the platform?	**Извинявайте, къде е изхода към влаковете?** [izvinʲávajte, kədé e íshoda kəm vlákovete?]

Does this train go to …?	**Този влак отива ли до …?** [tózi vlak otíva li do …?]
next train	**следващ влак** [slédvaʃt vlak]
When is the next train?	**Кога е следващият влак?** [kogá e slédvaʃtijat vlak?]
Where can I see the schedule?	**Къде мога да видя разписанието?** [kədé móga da vídʲa raspisánieto?]
From which platform?	**От кой перон?** [ot koj perón?]
When does the train arrive in …?	**Кога влакът пристига в …?** [kogá vlákət pristíga v …?]

Please help me.	**Помогнете ми, моля.** [pomognéte mi, mólʲa]
I'm looking for my seat.	**Аз търся мястото си.** [az térsʲa mʲástoto si]
We're looking for our seats.	**Ние търсим местата си.** [nie térsim mestáta si]

My seat is taken.	**Мястото ми е заето.** [mʲástoto mi e zaéto]
Our seats are taken.	**Местата ни са заети.** [mestáta ni sa zaéti]
I'm sorry but this is my seat.	**Извинявайте, но това е моето място.** [izvinʲávajte, no tová e móeto mʲásto]

Is this seat taken?

Това място свободно ли е?
[tová m'ásto svobódno li e?]

May I sit here?

Мога ли да седна тук?
[móga li da sédna tuk?]

On the train. Dialogue (No ticket)

Ticket, please.	**Билета ви, моля.** [biléta vi, mólʲa]
I don't have a ticket.	**Аз нямам билет.** [az nʲámam bilét]
I lost my ticket.	**Аз загубих билета си.** [az zagúbih biléta si]
I forgot my ticket at home.	**Аз забравих билета си в къщи.** [az zabrávih biléta si v kéʃti]
You can buy a ticket from me.	**Вие можете да си купите билет от мен.** [víe móʒete da si kúpite bilét ot men]
You will also have to pay a fine.	**Също така ще трябва да заплатите глоба.** [séʃto taká ʃte trʲábva da zaplátite glóba]
Okay.	**Добре.** [dobré]
Where are you going?	**Накъде пътувате?** [nakədé pətúvate?]
I'm going to ...	**Аз пътувам до ...** [az pətúvam do ...]
How much? I don't understand.	**Колко? Не разбирам.** [kólko? ne razbíram]
Write it down, please.	**Напишете, моля.** [napiʃéte, mólʲa]
Okay. Can I pay with a credit card?	**Добре. Мога ли да платя с карта?** [dobré. móga li da platʲá s kárta?]
Yes, you can.	**Да. Можете.** [da. móʒete]
Here's your receipt.	**Заповядайте, вашата квитанция.** [zapovʲádajte, vaʃata kvitántsija]
Sorry about the fine.	**Съжалявам за глобата.** [səʒalʲávam za glóbata]
That's okay. It was my fault.	**Няма нищо. Вината е моя.** [nʲáma níʃto. vináta e mója]
Enjoy your trip.	**Приятно пътуване.** [prijátno pətúvane]

Taxi

taxi	**такси** [táksi]
taxi driver	**таксист** [táksist]
to catch a taxi	**да взема такси** [da vzéma táksi]
taxi stand	**стоянка на такси** [stojánka na táksi]
Where can I get a taxi?	**Къде мога да взема такси?** [kədé móga da vzéma táksi?]

to call a taxi	**да повикам такси** [da povíkam táksi]
I need a taxi.	**Трябва ми такси.** [trʲábva mi táksi]
Right now.	**Точно сега.** [tótʃno segá]
What is your address (location)?	**Вашият адрес?** [váʃijat adrés?]
My address is ...	**Моят адрес е ...** [mójat adrés e ...]
Your destination?	**Къде отивате?** [kədé otívate?]
Excuse me, ...	**Извинете, ...** [izvinéte, ...]
Are you available?	**Свободни ли сте?** [svobódni li ste?]
How much is it to get to ...?	**Каква е цената до ...?** [kakvá e tsenáta do ...?]
Do you know where it is?	**Знаете ли, къде е това?** [znáete li, kədé e tová?]

Airport, please.	**До аерогарата, моля.** [do aerogárata, mólʲa]
Stop here, please.	**Спрете тук, моля.** [spréte tuk, mólʲa]
It's not here.	**Това не е тук.** [tová ne e tuk]
This is the wrong address.	**Това е неправилен адрес.** [tová e neprávilen adrés]
Turn left.	**наляво** [nalʲávo]
Turn right.	**надясно** [nadʲásno]

How much do I owe you?	**Колко ви дължа?** [kólko vi dəlʒá?]
I'd like a receipt, please.	**Дайте ми касов бон, моля.** [dájte mi kásov bon, mólʲa]
Keep the change.	**Задръжте рестото.** [zadréʒte réstoto]

Would you please wait for me?	**Изчакайте ме, моля.** [iztʃákajte me, mólʲa]
five minutes	**пет минути** [pet minúti]
ten minutes	**десет минути** [déset minúti]
fifteen minutes	**петнадесет минути** [petnádeset minúti]
twenty minutes	**двадесет минути** [dvádeset minúti]
half an hour	**половин час** [polóvin tʃas]

Hotel

Hello.	**Здравейте.** [zdravéjte]
My name is ...	**Казвам се ...** [kázvam se ...]
I have a reservation.	**Аз резервирах стая.** [az rezervírah stája]

I need ...	**Трябва ми ...** [trʲábva mi ...]
a single room	**единична стая** [edinítʃna stája]
a double room	**двойна стая** [dvójna stája]
How much is that?	**Колко струва?** [kólko strúva?]
That's a bit expensive.	**Това е малко скъпо.** [tová e málko sképo]

Do you have anything else?	**Имате ли още нещо?** [ímate li óʃte néʃto?]
I'll take it.	**Ще го взема.** [ʃte go vzéma]
I'll pay in cash.	**Ще платя в брой.** [ʃte plátʲa v broj]

I've got a problem.	**Аз имам проблем.** [az ímam problém]
My ... is broken.	**Моят /моята/ ... е счупен /счупена/.** [mójat /mójata/ ... e stʃúpen /stʃúpena/]
My ... is out of order.	**Моят /моята/ ... не работи** [mójat /mójata/ ... ne ráboti]
TV	**моят телевизор** [mójat televízor]
air conditioner	**моят климатик** [mójat klímatik]
tap	**моят кран** [mójat kran]

shower	**моят душ** [mójat duʃ]
sink	**моята мивка** [mójata mífka]
safe	**моят сейф** [mójat sejf]

door lock	**моята ключалка** [mójata klʲútʃálka]
electrical outlet	**моят контакт** [mójat kontákt]
hairdryer	**моят сешоар** [mójat seʃoár]

I don't have …	**Нямам …** [nʲámam …]
water	**вода** [vodá]
light	**ток** [tok]
electricity	**електричество** [elektrítʃestvo]

Can you give me …?	**Може ли да ми дадете …?** [móʒe li da mi dadéte …?]
a towel	**хавлия** [havlíja]
a blanket	**одеяло** [odejálo]
slippers	**чехли** [tʃéhli]
a robe	**халат** [halát]
shampoo	**шампоан** [ʃampoán]
soap	**сапун** [sapún]

I'd like to change rooms.	**Бих искал /искала/** **да сменя стаята си.** [bih ískal /ískala/ da smenʲá stájata si]
I can't find my key.	**Не мога да намеря ключа си.** [ne móga da namérʲa klʲútʃa si]
Could you open my room, please?	**Отворете моята стая, моля.** [otvórete mójata stája, mólʲa]
Who's there?	**Кой е?** [koj e?]
Come in!	**Влезте!** [vlézte!]
Just a minute!	**Една минута!** [edná minúta!]

Not right now, please.	**Моля, не сега.** [mólʲa, ne segá]
Come to my room, please.	**Влезте при мен, моля.** [vlézte pri men, mólʲa]

I'd like to order food service.

Бих искал /искала/ да поръчам храна за стаята.
[bih ískal /ískala/ da póretʃam hraná za stájata]

My room number is ...

Номерът на стаята ми е ....
[nómerǝt na stájata mi e ....]

I'm leaving ...

Заминавам ...
[zaminávam ...]

We're leaving ...

Ние заминаваме ...
[nie zaminávame ...]

right now

сега
[segá]

this afternoon

днес след обяд
[dnes slet obʲát]

tonight

днес вечерта
[dnes vetʃertá]

tomorrow

утре
[útre]

tomorrow morning

утре сутринта
[útre sutrínta]

tomorrow evening

утре вечер
[útre vétʃer]

the day after tomorrow

вдругиден
[vdrúgiden]

I'd like to pay.

Бих искал /искала/ да заплатя.
[bih ískal /ískala/ da zaplatʲá]

Everything was wonderful.

Всичко беше отлично.
[fsítʃko béʃe otlítʃno]

Where can I get a taxi?

Къде мога да взема такси?
[kǝdé móga da vzéma táksi?]

Would you call a taxi for me, please?

Повикайте ми такси, моля.
[povikájte mi táksi, mólʲa]

Restaurant

Can I look at the menu, please?	**Мога ли да видя менюто ви?** [móga li da vídʲa menʲúto vi?]
Table for one.	**Маса за един човек.** [mása za edín ʧovék]
There are two (three, four) of us.	**Ние сме двама (трима, четирима).** [nie sme dváma (tríma, ʧetírima)]

Smoking	**За пушачи** [za puʃáʧi]
No smoking	**За непушачи** [za nepuʃáʧi]
Excuse me! (addressing a waiter)	**Ако обичате!** [ako obiʧate!]
menu	**меню** [menʲú]
wine list	**Карта на виното** [kárta na vínoto]
The menu, please.	**Менюто, моля.** [menʲúto, mólʲa]

Are you ready to order?	**Готови ли сте да поръчате?** [gotóvi li ste da poréʧate?]
What will you have?	**Какво ще поръчате?** [kakvó ʃte poréʧate?]
I'll have ...	**Аз искам ....** [az ískam ....]

I'm a vegetarian.	**Аз съм вегетарианец /вегетарианка/.** [az səm vegetariánets /vegetariánka/]
meat	**месо** [mesó]
fish	**риба** [ríba]
vegetables	**зеленчуци** [zelenʧútsi]
Do you have vegetarian dishes?	**Имате ли вегетариански ястия?** [ímate li vegetariánski jástija?]
I don't eat pork.	**Аз не ям свинско.** [az ne jam svínsko]
Band-Aid	**Той /тя/ не яде месо.** [toj /tʲa/ ne jadé mesó]
I am allergic to ...	**Имам алергия към ...** [ímam alérgija kəm ...]

Would you please bring me …

Донесете ми, моля …
[doneséte mi, mólʲa …]

salt | pepper | sugar

сол | пипер | захар
[sol | pipér | záhar]

coffee | tea | dessert

кафе | чай | десерт
[kafé | tʃaj | desért]

water | sparkling | plain

вода | газирана | негазирана
[vodá | gazírana | negazírana]

a spoon | fork | knife

лъжица | вилица | нож
[ləʒítsa | vílitsa | noʒ]

a plate | napkin

чиния | салфетка
[tʃiníja | salfétka]

Enjoy your meal!

Приятен апетит!
[prijáten apetít!]

One more, please.

Донесете още, моля.
[doneséte óʃte, mólʲa]

It was very delicious.

Беше много вкусно.
[béʃe mnógo fkúsno]

check | change | tip

сметка | ресто | бакшиш
[smétka | résto | bakʃíʃ]

Check, please.
(Could I have the check, please?)

Сметката, моля.
[smétkata, mólʲa]

Can I pay by credit card?

Мога ли да платя с карта?
[móga li da platʲá s kárta?]

I'm sorry, there's a mistake here.

Извинявайте, тук има грешка.
[izvinʲávajte, tuk íma gréʃka]

Shopping

Can I help you?	**Мога ли да ви помогна?** [móga li da vi pomógna?]
Do you have ...?	**Имате ли ...?** [ímate li ...?]
I'm looking for ...	**Аз търся ...** [az tǝ́rsʲa ...]
I need ...	**Трябва ми ...** [trʲábva mi ...]
I'm just looking.	**Само гледам.** [sámo glédam]
We're just looking.	**Ние само гледаме.** [nie sámo glédame]
I'll come back later.	**Ще дойда по-късно.** [ʃte dójda po-kǝ́sno]
We'll come back later.	**Ние ще дойдем по-късно.** [nie ʃte dójdem po-kǝ́sno]
discounts | sale	**намаления | разпродажба** [namalénija | rasprodáʒba]
Would you please show me ...	**Покажете ми, моля ...** [pokaʒéte mi, mólʲa ...]
Would you please give me ...	**Дайте ми, моля ...** [dájte mi, mólʲa ...]
Can I try it on?	**Може ли да пробвам това?** [móʒe li da próbvam tová?]
Excuse me, where's the fitting room?	**Извинявайте, къде може да пробвам това?** [izvinʲávajte, kǝdé móʒe da próbvam tová?]
Which color would you like?	**Какъв цвят желаете?** [kakǝ́v tsvʲat ʒeláete?]
size | length	**размер | ръст** [razmér | rǝst]
How does it fit?	**Стана ли ви?** [stána li vi?]
How much is it?	**Колко струва това?** [kólko strúva tová?]
That's too expensive.	**Това е много скъпо.** [tová e mnógo skǝ́po]
I'll take it.	**Ще взема това.** [ʃte vzéma tová]

Excuse me, where do I pay?	**Извинявайте, къде е касата?** [izvin'ávajte, kədé e kásata?]
Will you pay in cash or credit card?	**Как ще плащате?** **В брой или с карта?** [kak ʃte pláʃtate? v broj íli s kárta?]
In cash | with credit card	**в брой | с карта** [v broj | s kárta]

Do you want the receipt?	**Трябва ли ви касов бон?** [tr'ábva li vi kásov bon?]
Yes, please.	**Да, бъдете така добър.** [da, bədéte taká dobér]
No, it's OK.	**Не, не трябва. Благодаря.** [ne, ne tr'ábva. blagodar'á]
Thank you. Have a nice day!	**Благодаря. Всичко хубаво!** [blagodar'á. fsíʧko húbavo!]

In town

Excuse me, ...	**Извинете, моля ...** [izvinéte, mólʲa ...]
I'm looking for ...	**Аз търся ...** [az térsʲa ...]
the subway	**метрото** [metróto]
my hotel	**хотела си** [hotéla si]
the movie theater	**киното** [kínoto]
a taxi stand	**стоянката на такси** [stojánkata na táksi]
an ATM	**банкомат** [bankomát]
a foreign exchange office	**обмяна на валута** [obmʲána na valúta]
an internet café	**интернет-кафе** [internét-kafé]
... street	**улица ...** [úlitsa ...]
this place	**ето това място** [eto tová mʲásto]
Do you know where ... is?	**Знаете ли, къде се намира ...?** [znáete li, kədé se namíra ...?]
Which street is this?	**Как се нарича тази улица?** [kak se narítʃa tázi úlitsa?]
Show me where we are right now.	**Покажете, къде сме сега.** [pokaʒéte, kədé sme segá]
Can I get there on foot?	**Ще стигна ли дотам пеша?** [ʃte stígna li dotám péʃa?]
Do you have a map of the city?	**Имате ли карта на града?** [ímate li kárta na gradá?]
How much is a ticket to get in?	**Колко струва билет за вход?** [kólko strúva bilét za vhot?]
Can I take pictures here?	**Тук може ли да се снима?** [tuk móʒe li da se snimá?]
Are you open?	**Отворено ли е?** [otvóreno li e?]

When do you open?

В колко отваряте?
[v kólko otvár'ate?]

When do you close?

До колко часа работите?
[do kólko ʧása rábotite?]

Money

money	**пари** [parí]
cash	**пари в брой** [parí v broj]
paper money	**книжни пари** [kníʒni parí]
loose change	**дребни пари** [drébni parí]
check | change | tip	**сметка | ресто | бакшиш** [smétka | résto | bakʃíʃ]
credit card	**кредитна карта** [kréditna kárta]
wallet	**портмоне** [portmoné]
to buy	**да купя** [da kúpʲa]
to pay	**да платя** [da platʲá]
fine	**глоба** [glóba]
free	**безплатно** [besplátno]
Where can I buy ...?	**Къде мога да купя ...?** [kədé móga da kúpʲa ...?]
Is the bank open now?	**Отворена ли е банката сега ?** [otvórena li e bánkata segá ?]
When does it open?	**В колко се отваря?** [v kólko se otvárʲa?]
When does it close?	**До колко часа работи?** [do kólko ʧása ráboti?]
How much?	**Колко?** [kólko?]
How much is this?	**Колко струва?** [kólko strúva?]
That's too expensive.	**Това е много скъпо.** [tová e mnógo sképo]
Excuse me, where do I pay?	**Извинявайте, къде е касата?** [izvinʲávajte, kədé e kásata?]
Check, please.	**Сметката, моля.** [smétkata, mólʲa]

Can I pay by credit card? **Мога ли да платя с карта?**
[móga li da plat'á s kárta?]

Is there an ATM here? **Тук има ли банкомат?**
[tuk íma li bankomát?]

I'm looking for an ATM. **Трябва ми банкомат.**
[tr'ábva mi bankomát]

I'm looking for a foreign exchange office. **Аз търся обмяна на валута.**
[az tórs'a obm'ána na valúta]

I'd like to change … **Бих искал да сменя …**
[bih ískal da smen'á …]

What is the exchange rate? **Какъв е курсът?**
[kakóv e kúrsət?]

Do you need my passport? **Трябва ли ви паспортът ми?**
[tr'ábva li vi paspórtət mi?]

Time

What time is it?	**Колко е часът?** [kólko e ʧasét?]
When?	**Кога?** [kogá?]
At what time?	**В колко?** [v kólko?]
now	later	after …	**сега	по-късно	след …** [segá	po-késno	slet …]
one o'clock	**един часа** [edín ʧása]
one fifteen	**един часа и петнадесет минути** [edín ʧása i petnádeset minúti]
one thirty	**един часа и тридесет минути** [edín ʧása i trídeset minúti]
one forty-five	**два без петнадесет** [dva bez petnádeset]
one	two	three	**един	два	три** [edín	dva	tri]
four	five	six	**четири	пет	шест** [ʧétiri	pet	ʃest]
seven	eight	nine	**седем	осем	девет** [sédem	ósem	dévet]
ten	eleven	twelve	**десет	единадесет	дванадесет** [déset	edinádeset	dvanádeset]
in …	**след …** [slet …]
five minutes	**пет минути** [pet minúti]
ten minutes	**десет минути** [déset minúti]
fifteen minutes	**петнадесет минути** [petnádeset minúti]
twenty minutes	**двадесет минути** [dvádeset minúti]
half an hour	**половин час** [polóvin ʧas]
an hour	**един час** [edín ʧas]

in the morning	**сутринта** [sutrínta]
early in the morning	**рано сутринта** [ráno sutrínta]
this morning	**днес сутринта** [dnes sutrínta]
tomorrow morning	**утре сутринта** [útre sutrínta]
in the middle of the day	**на обяд** [na obʲád]
in the afternoon	**след обяд** [slet obʲát]
in the evening	**вечерта** [vetʃertá]
tonight	**днес вечерта** [dnes vetʃertá]
at night	**през нощта** [prez noʃtá]
yesterday	**вчера** [vtʃéra]
today	**днес** [dnes]
tomorrow	**утре** [útre]
the day after tomorrow	**вдругиден** [vdrúgiden]
What day is it today?	**Какъв ден е днес?** [kakév den e dnes?]
It's …	**Днес е …** [dnes e …]
Monday	**понеделник** [ponedélnik]
Tuesday	**вторник** [ftórnik]
Wednesday	**сряда** [srʲáda]
Thursday	**четвъртък** [tʃetvértək]
Friday	**петък** [pétək]
Saturday	**събота** [sébota]
Sunday	**неделя** [nedélʲa]

Greetings. Introductions

Hello.
Здравейте.
[zdravéjte]

Pleased to meet you.
Радвам се, че се запознахме.
[rádvam se, t͡ʃe se zapoznáhme]

Me too.
И аз.
[i az]

I'd like you to meet …
Запознайте се. Това е …
[zapoznájte se. tová e …]

Nice to meet you.
Много ми е приятно.
[mnógo mi e prijátno]

How are you?
Как сте?
[kak ste?]

My name is …
Казвам се …
[kázvam se …]

His name is …
Той се казва …
[toj se kázva …]

Her name is …
Тя се казва …
[tʲa se kázva …]

What's your name?
Как се казвате?
[kak se kázvate?]

What's his name?
Как се казва той?
[kak se kázva toj?]

What's her name?
Как се казва тя?
[kak se kázva tʲa?]

What's your last name?
Как ви е фамилията?
[kak vi e famílijata?]

You can call me …
Наричайте ме …
[narít͡ʃajte me …]

Where are you from?
Откъде сте?
[otkədé ste?]

I'm from …
Аз съм от …
[az səm ot …]

What do you do for a living?
Като какъв работите?
[kató kakév rábotite?]

Who is this?
Кой сте?
[koj ste?]

Who is he?
Кой е той?
[koj e toj?]

Who is she?
Коя е тя?
[kojá e tʲa?]

Who are they?
Кои са те?
[koi sa te?]

This is ...   **Това е ...**
[tová e ...]

my friend (masc.)   **моят приятел**
[mójat prijátel]

my friend (fem.)   **моята приятелка**
[mójata prijátelka]

my husband   **моят мъж**
[mójat meʒ]

my wife   **моята жена**
[mójata ʒená]

my father   **моят баща**
[mójat baʃtá]

my mother   **моята майка**
[mójata májka]

my brother   **моят брат**
[mójat brat]

my sister   **моята сестра**
[mójata sestrá]

my son   **моят син**
[mójat sin]

my daughter   **моята дъщеря**
[mójata deʃterʲá]

This is our son.   **Това е нашият син.**
[tová e náʃijat sin]

This is our daughter.   **Това е нашата дъщеря.**
[tová e náʃata deʃterʲá]

These are my children.   **Това са моите деца.**
[tová sa móite detsá]

These are our children.   **Това са нашите деца.**
[tová sa náʃite detsá]

Farewells

Good bye!
Довиждане!
[dovíʒdane!]

Bye! (inform.)
Чао!
[tʃao!]

See you tomorrow.
До утре!
[do útre!]

See you soon.
До срещата!
[do sréʃtata!]

See you at seven.
Ще се срещнем в седем.
[ʃte se sréʃtnem v sédem]

Have fun!
Забавлявайте се!
[zabavlʲávajte se!]

Talk to you later.
Ще поговорим по-късно.
[ʃte pogovórim po-kásno]

Have a nice weekend.
Успешен уикенд!
[uspéʃen uіkend!]

Good night.
Лека нощ.
[léka noʃt]

It's time for me to go.
Сега трябва да тръгвам.
[segá trʲábva da trégvam]

I have to go.
Трябва да тръгвам.
[trʲábva da trégvam]

I will be right back.
Сега ще се върна.
[segá ʃte se vérna]

It's late.
Вече е късно.
[vétʃe e kásno]

I have to get up early.
Трябва рано да ставам.
[trʲábva ráno da stávam]

I'm leaving tomorrow.
Аз заминавам утре.
[az zaminávam útre]

We're leaving tomorrow.
Ние утре заминаваме.
[nie útre zaminávame]

Have a nice trip!
Щастливо пътуване!
[ʃtastlívo pətúvane!]

It was nice meeting you.
Беше ми приятно да се запознаем.
[béʃe mi prijátno da se zapoznáem]

It was nice talking to you.
Беше ми приятно да поговоря с вас.
[béʃe mi prijátno da pogovórʲa s vas]

Thanks for everything.
Благодаря за всичко.
[blagodarʲá za fsítʃko]

I had a very good time.	**Прекрасно прекарах времето.** [prekrásno prekárah vrémeto]
We had a very good time.	**Ние прекрасно прекарахме времето.** [nie prekrásno prekárahme vrémeto]
It was really great.	**Всичкото беше страхотно.** [fsítʃkoto béʃe strahótno]
I'm going to miss you.	**Ще скучая.** [ʃte skutʃája]
We're going to miss you.	**Ние ще скучаем.** [nie ʃte skutʃáem]
Good luck!	**Късмет! Успех!** [kəsmét! uspéh!]
Say hi to …	**Предайте поздрави на …** [predájte pózdravi na …]

Foreign language

I don't understand.
Аз не разбирам.
[az ne razbíram]

Write it down, please.
Напишете това, моля.
[napiʃéte tová, mólʲa]

Do you speak ...?
Знаете ли ...?
[znáete li ...?]

I speak a little bit of ...
Малко знам ...
[málko znam ...]

English
английски
[anglíjski]

Turkish
турски
[túrski]

Arabic
арабски
[arápski]

French
френски
[frénski]

German
немски
[némski]

Italian
италиански
[italiánski]

Spanish
испански
[ispánski]

Portuguese
португалски
[portugálski]

Chinese
китайски
[kitájski]

Japanese
японски
[japónski]

Can you repeat that, please.
Повторете, моля.
[poftoréte, mólʲa]

I understand.
Аз разбирам.
[az razbíram]

I don't understand.
Аз не разбирам.
[az ne razbíram]

Please speak more slowly.
Говорете по-бавно, моля.
[govórete po-bávno, mólʲa]

Is that correct? (Am I saying it right?)
Това правилно ли е?
[tová právilno li e?]

What is this? (What does this mean?)
Какво е това?
[kakvó e tová?]

Apologies

Excuse me, please.	**Извинете, моля.** [izvinéte, mólʲa]
I'm sorry.	**Съжалявам.** [səʒalʲávam]
I'm really sorry.	**Много съжалявам.** [mnógo səʒalʲávam]
Sorry, it's my fault.	**Виновен съм, вината е моя.** [vinóven səm, vináta e mója]
My mistake.	**Грешката е моя.** [greʃkata e mója]
May I ...?	**Мога ли ...?** [móga li ...?]
Do you mind if I ...?	**Имате ли нещо против, ако аз ...?** [ímate li néʃto protív, akó az ...?]
It's OK.	**Няма нищо.** [nʲáma níʃto]
It's all right.	**Всичко е наред.** [fsíʧko e naréd]
Don't worry about it.	**Не се безпокойте.** [ne se bespokójte]

Agreement

Yes.	**Да.** [da]
Yes, sure.	**Да, разбира се.** [da, razbíra se]
OK (Good!)	**Добре!** [dobré!]
Very well.	**Много добре!** [mnógo dobré!]
Certainly!	**Разбира се!** [razbíra se!]
I agree.	**Съгласен /съгласна/ съм.** [səglásen /səglásna/ səm]

That's correct.	**Вярно.** [vʲárno]
That's right.	**Правилно.** [právilno]
You're right.	**Прав /права/ сте.** [prav /práva/ ste]
I don't mind.	**Не възразявам.** [ne vəzrazʲávam]
Absolutely right.	**Абсолютно вярно.** [absolʲútno vʲárno]

It's possible.	**Това е възможно.** [tová e vəzmóʒno]
That's a good idea.	**Това е добра идея.** [tová e dobrá idéja]
I can't say no.	**Не мога да откажа.** [ne móga da otkáʒa]
I'd be happy to.	**Ще се радвам.** [ʃte se rádvam]
With pleasure.	**С удоволствие.** [s udovólstvie]

Refusal. Expressing doubt

No.	**Не.** [ne]
Certainly not.	**Не, разбира се.** [ne, razbíra se]
I don't agree.	**Аз не съм съгласен /съгласна/.** [az ne səm səglásen /səglásna/]
I don't think so.	**Аз не мисля така.** [az ne mísľa taká]
It's not true.	**Това не е вярно.** [tová ne e vʲárno]
You are wrong.	**Грешите.** [greʃíte]
I think you are wrong.	**Мисля, че грешите.** [mísľa, ʧe greʃíte]
I'm not sure.	**Не съм сигурен /сигурна/.** [ne səm síguren /sígurna/]
It's impossible.	**Това не е възможно.** [tová ne e vəzmóʒno]
Nothing of the kind (sort)!	**Нищо подобно!** [niʃto podóbno!]
The exact opposite.	**Напротив!** [naprótiv!]
I'm against it.	**Аз съм против.** [az səm protív]
I don't care.	**На мен ми е все едно.** [na men mi e fse ednó]
I have no idea.	**Нямам представа.** [nʲámam pretstáva]
I doubt it.	**Съмнявам се, че е така.** [səmnʲávam se, ʧe e taká]
Sorry, I can't.	**Извинете ме, аз не мога.** [izvinéte me, az ne móga]
Sorry, I don't want to.	**Извинете ме, аз не искам.** [izvinéte me, az neískam]
Thank you, but I don't need this.	**Благодаря, това не ми трябва.** [blagodarʲá, tová ne mi trʲábva]
It's getting late.	**Вече е късно.** [véʧe e kәsno]

I have to get up early.

Трябва рано да ставам.
[triábva ráno da stávam]

I don't feel well.

Чувствам се зле.
[ʧúfstvam se zle]

Expressing gratitude

Thank you.	**Благодаря.** [blagodar'á]
Thank you very much.	**Много благодаря.** [mnógo blagodar'á]
I really appreciate it.	**Много съм признателен /признателна/.** [mnógo səm priznátelen /priznátelna/]
I'm really grateful to you.	**Много съм ви благодарен /благодарна/.** [mnógo səm vi blagodáren /blagodárna/]
We are really grateful to you.	**Ние сме ви благодарни.** [nie sme vi blagodárni]
Thank you for your time.	**Благодаря ви, че отделихте време.** [blagodar'á vi, ʧe otdelíhte vréme]
Thanks for everything.	**Благодаря за всичко.** [blagodar'á za fsíʧko]
Thank you for ...	**Благодаря за ...** [blagodar'á za ...]
your help	**вашата помощ** [váʃata pómoʃt]
a nice time	**хубавото време** [húbavoto vréme]
a wonderful meal	**чудната храна** [ʧúdnata hraná]
a pleasant evening	**приятната вечер** [prijátnata véʧer]
a wonderful day	**прекрасния ден** [prekrásnija den]
an amazing journey	**интересната екскурзия** [interésnata ekskúrzija]
Don't mention it.	**Няма за що.** [n'áma za ʃto]
You are welcome.	**Моля.** [mól'a]
Any time.	**Винаги моля.** [vínagi mól'a]
My pleasure.	**Радвам се, че помогнах.** [rádvam se, ʧe pomógnah]

Forget it.

Забравете.
[zabravéte]

Don't worry about it.

Не се безпокойте.
[ne se bespokójte]

Congratulations. Best wishes

Congratulations!
Поздравявам!
[pozdrav'ávam!]

Happy birthday!
Честит рожден ден!
[tʃestít roʒdén den!]

Merry Christmas!
Весела Коледа!
[vésela kóleda!]

Happy New Year!
Честита Нова година!
[tʃestíta nóva godína!]

Happy Easter!
Честит Великден!
[tʃestít velíkden!]

Happy Hanukkah!
Честита Ханука!
[tʃestíta hánuka!]

I'd like to propose a toast.
Имам тост.
[ímam tost]

Cheers!
За вашето здраве!
[za váʃeto zdráve!]

Let's drink to ...!
Да пием за ...!
[da piém za ...!]

To our success!
За нашия успех!
[za náʃija uspéh!]

To your success!
За вашия успех!
[za váʃija uspéh!]

Good luck!
Късмет!
[kəsmét!]

Have a nice day!
Приятен ден!
[prijáten den!]

Have a good holiday!
Хубава почивка!
[húbava potʃífka!]

Have a safe journey!
Успешно пътуване!
[uspéʃno pətúvane!]

I hope you get better soon!
Желая ви скорошно оздравяване!
[ʒelája vi skóroʃno ozdrav'ávane!]

Socializing

Why are you sad?	**Защо сте разстроени?** [zaʃtó ste rasstróeni?]
Smile! Cheer up!	**Усмихнете се!** [usmihnéte se!]
Are you free tonight?	**Заети ли сте днес вечерта?** [zaéti li ste dnes vetʃertá?]
May I offer you a drink?	**Мога ли да ви предложа едно питие?** [móga li da vi predlóʒa ednó pitié?]
Would you like to dance?	**Искате ли да танцувате?** [ískate li da tantsúvate?]
Let's go to the movies.	**Да отидем ли на кино?** [da otídem li na kíno?]
May I invite you to …?	**Мога ли да ви поканя на …?** [móga li da vi pokánʲa na …?]
a restaurant	**ресторант** [restoránt]
the movies	**кино** [kíno]
the theater	**театър** [teátər]
go for a walk	**на разходка** [na rashótka]
At what time?	**В колко?** [v kólko?]
tonight	**днес вечерта** [dnes vetʃertá]
at six	**в 6 часа** [v ʃest tʃasá]
at seven	**в 7 часа** [v sédem tʃasá]
at eight	**в 8 часа** [v ósem tʃasá]
at nine	**в 9 часа** [v dévet tʃasá]
Do you like it here?	**Харесва ли ви тук?** [harésva li vi tuk?]
Are you here with someone?	**С някой ли сте тук?** [s nʲákoj li ste tuk?]

I'm with my friend. | **Аз съм с приятел /приятелка/.**
[az səm s prijátel /prijátelka/]

I'm with my friends. | **Аз съм с приятели.**
[az səm s prijáteli]

No, I'm alone. | **Аз съм сам /сама/.**
[az səm sam /samá/]

Do you have a boyfriend? | **Имаш ли приятел?**
[ímaʃ li prijátel?]

I have a boyfriend. | **Аз имам приятел.**
[az ímam prijátel]

Do you have a girlfriend? | **Имаш ли приятелка?**
[ímaʃ li prijátelka?]

I have a girlfriend. | **Аз имам гадже.**
[az ímam gádʒe]

Can I see you again? | **Ще се видим ли още?**
[ʃte se vídim li oʃté?]

Can I call you? | **Мога ли да ти се обадя?**
[móga li da ti se obádʲa?]

Call me. (Give me a call.) | **Обади ми се.**
[obádi mi se]

What's your number? | **Какъв ти е номерът?**
[kakév ti e nómerət?]

I miss you. | **Липсваш ми.**
[lípsvaʃ mi]

You have a beautiful name. | **Имате много красиво име.**
[ímate mnógo krasívo íme]

I love you. | **Аз те обичам.**
[az te obítʃam]

Will you marry me? | **Омъжи се за мен.**
[oméʒi se za men]

You're kidding! | **Шегувате се!**
[ʃegúvate se!]

I'm just kidding. | **Аз само се шегувам.**
[az sámo se ʃegúvam]

Are you serious? | **Сериозно ли говорите?**
[seriózno li govórite?]

I'm serious. | **Сериозен /сериозна/ съм.**
[seriózen /seriózna/ səm]

Really?! | **Наистина ли?!**
[naístina li?!]

It's unbelievable! | **Това е невероятно!**
[tová e neverojátno!]

I don't believe you. | **Не ви вярвам.**
[ne vi vʲárvam]

I can't. | **Аз не мога.**
[az ne móga]

I don't know. | **Аз не знам.**
[az ne znam]

I don't understand you.

Аз не ви разбирам.
[az ne vi razbíram]

Please go away.

Вървете си, моля.
[vərvéte si, mólʲa]

Leave me alone!

Оставете ме на мира!
[ostávete me na mirá!]

I can't stand him.

Не го понасям.
[ne go ponásʲam]

You are disgusting!

Отвратителен сте!
[otvratítelen ste!]

I'll call the police!

Ще повикам полиция!
[ʃte póvikam polítsija!]

Sharing impressions. Emotions

I like it.	Това ми харесва. [tová mi harésva]
Very nice.	Много мило. [mnógo mílo]
That's great!	Това е страхотно! [tová e strahótno!]
It's not bad.	Не е лошо. [ne e lóʃo]

I don't like it.	Това не ми харесва. [tová ne mi harésva]
It's not good.	Това не е добре. [tová ne e dobré]
It's bad.	Това е лошо. [tová e lóʃo]
It's very bad.	Това е много лошо. [tová e mnógo lóʃo]
It's disgusting.	Това е отвратително. [tová e otvratítelno]

I'm happy.	Щастлив /щастлива/ съм. [ʃtastlív /ʃtastlíva/ səm]
I'm content.	Доволен /доволна/ съм. [dovólen /dovólna/ səm]
I'm in love.	Влюбен /влюбена/ съм. [vlʲúben /vlʲúbena/ səm]
I'm calm.	Спокоен /спокойна/ съм. [spokóen /spokójna/ səm]
I'm bored.	Скучно ми е. [skúʧno mi e]

I'm tired.	Аз се измморих. [az se izmoríh]
I'm sad.	Тъжно ми е. [téʒno mi e]
I'm frightened.	Уплашен /уплашена/ съм. [upláʃen /upláʃena/ səm]

I'm angry.	Ядосвам се. [jadósvam se]
I'm worried.	Вълнувам се. [vəlnúvam se]
I'm nervous.	Аз нервнича. [az nérvniʧa]

I'm jealous. (envious)

Аз завиждам.
[az zavíʒdam]

I'm surprised.

Учуден /учудена/ съм.
[utʃúden /utʃúdena/ səm]

I'm perplexed.

Аз съм объркан /объркана/.
[az səm obə́rkan /obə́rkana/]

Problems. Accidents

I've got a problem.	**Аз имам проблем.**
	[az ímam problém]
We've got a problem.	**Ние имаме проблем.**
	[nie ímame problém]
I'm lost.	**Аз се заблудих.**
	[az se zablúdih]
I missed the last bus (train).	**Аз закъснях за последния автобус (влак).**
	[az zakəsnʲáh za poslédniʲa aftobús (vlak)]
I don't have any money left.	**Не ми останаха никакви пари.**
	[ne mi ostánaha níkakvi parí]

I've lost my ...	**Аз загубих ...**
	[az zagúbih ...]
Someone stole my ...	**Откраднаха ми ...**
	[otkrádnaha mi ...]
passport	**паспорта**
	[paspórta]
wallet	**портмонето**
	[portmonéto]
papers	**документите**
	[dokuméntite]
ticket	**билета**
	[biléta]

money	**парите**
	[paríte]
handbag	**чантата**
	[ʧántata]
camera	**фотоапарата**
	[fotoaparáta]
laptop	**лаптопа**
	[laptópa]
tablet computer	**таблета**
	[tabléta]
mobile phone	**телефона**
	[telefóna]

Help me!	**Помогнете!**
	[pomognéte!]
What's happened?	**Какво се случи?**
	[kakvó se sluʧí?]

fire

пожар
[poʒár]

shooting

стрелба
[strelbá]

murder

убийство
[ubíjstvo]

explosion

взрив
[vzriv]

fight

бой
[boj]

Call the police!

Извикайте полиция!
[izvikájte polítsija!]

Please hurry up!

Моля, по-бързо!
[mólʲa, po-bérzo!]

I'm looking for the police station.

Аз търся полицейски участък.
[az térsʲa politséjski uˈtʃastək]

I need to make a call.

Трябва да се обадя.
[trʲábva da se obádʲa]

May I use your phone?

Мога ли да се обадя?
[móga li da se obádʲa?]

I've been …

Мен ме …
[men me …]

mugged

ограбиха
[ográbiha]

robbed

обраха
[obráha]

raped

изнасилиха
[iznasíliha]

attacked (beaten up)

пребиха
[prebíha]

Are you all right?

Всичко ли е наред?
[fsítʃko li e naréd?]

Did you see who it was?

Видяхте ли, кой беше?
[vidʲáhte li, koj béʃe?]

Would you be able to recognize the person?

Ще можете ли да го познаете?
[ʃte móʒete li da go poznáete?]

Are you sure?

Сигурен /сигурна/ ли сте?
[síguren /sígurna/ li ste?]

Please calm down.

Моля, да се успокоите.
[mólʲa, da se uspokóite]

Take it easy!

По-спокойно!
[po-spokójno!]

Don't worry!

Не се безпокойте.
[ne se bespokójte]

Everything will be fine.

Всичко ще се оправи.
[fsítʃko ʃte se oprávi]

Everything's all right.

Всичко е наред.
[fsítʃko e naréd]

Come here, please.

Елате, моля.
[eláte, mólʲa]

I have some questions for you.

Имам няколко въпроса към Вас.
[ímam nʲakólko vəprósa kəm vas]

Wait a moment, please.

Изчакайте, моля.
[iztʃákajte, mólʲa]

Do you have any I.D.?

Имате ли документи?
[ímate li dokuménti?]

Thanks. You can leave now.

Благодаря. Свободни сте.
[blagodarʲá. svobódni ste]

Hands behind your head!

Ръцете зад тила!
[rətséte zat tíla!]

You're under arrest!

Арестуван /арестувана/ сте!
[arestúvan /arestúvana/ ste!]

Health problems

Please help me.	**Помогнете, моля.** [pomognéte, mólʲa]
I don't feel well.	**Лошо ми е.** [lóʃo mi e]
My husband doesn't feel well.	**На мъжа ми му е лошо.** [na məʒá mi mu e lóʃo]
My son …	**На сина ми …** [na siná mi …]
My father …	**На баща ми …** [na baʃtá mi …]
My wife doesn't feel well.	**На жена ми и е лошо.** [na ʒená mi i e lóʃo]
My daughter …	**На дъщеря ми …** [na dəʃterʲá mi …]
My mother …	**На майка ми …** [na májka mi …]
I've got a …	**Боли ме …** [bolí me …]
headache	**главата** [glaváta]
sore throat	**гърлото** [gə́rloto]
stomach ache	**корема** [koréma]
toothache	**зъба** [zə́ba]
I feel dizzy.	**Ви е ми се свят.** [vi e mi se svʲat]
He has a fever.	**Той има температура.** [toj íma temperatúra]
She has a fever.	**Тя има температура.** [tʲa íma temperatúra]
I can't breathe.	**Аз не мога да дишам.** [az ne móga da díʃam]
I'm short of breath.	**Аз се задъхвам.** [az se zadə́hvam]
I am asthmatic.	**Аз съм астматик.** [az səm astmatík]
I am diabetic.	**Аз съм диабетик.** [az səm diabetík]

I can't sleep.
Имам безсъние.
[ímam bessénie]

food poisoning
хранително отравяне
[hranítelno otráv'ane]

It hurts here.
Тук ме боли.
[tuk me bolí]

Help me!
Помогнете!
[pomognéte!]

I am here!
Аз съм тук!
[az səm tuk!]

We are here!
Ние сме тук!
[nie sme tuk!]

Get me out of here!
Извадете ме!
[izvadéte me!]

I need a doctor.
Трябва ми лекар.
[tr'ábva mi lékar]

I can't move.
Не мога да мърдам.
[ne móga da mérdam]

I can't move my legs.
Не си чувствам краката.
[ne si tʃúfstvam krakáta]

I have a wound.
Аз съм ранен /ранена/.
[az səm ránen /ránena/]

Is it serious?
Сериозно ли е?
[seriózno li e?]

My documents are in my pocket.
Документите ми са в джоба.
[dokuméntite mi sa v dʒóba]

Calm down!
Успокойте се!
[uspokójte se!]

May I use your phone?
Мога ли да се обадя?
[móga li da se obád'a?]

Call an ambulance!
Повикайте бърза помощ!
[povikájte bérza pómoʃt!]

It's urgent!
Това е спешно!
[tová e spéʃno!]

It's an emergency!
Това е много спешно!
[tová e mnógo spéʃno!]

Please hurry up!
Моля, по-бързо!
[mól'a, po-bérzo!]

Would you please call a doctor?
Повикайте лекар, моля.
[povikájte lékar, mól'a]

Where is the hospital?
Кажете, моля, къде е болницата?
[kaʒéte, mól'a, kədé e bólnitsata?]

How are you feeling?
Как се чувствате?
[kak se tʃúfstvate?]

Are you all right?
Всичко ли е наред?
[fsítʃko li e naréd?]

What's happened?
Какво се случи?
[kakvó se slutʃí?]

I feel better now.

Вече ми е по-добре.
[vétʃe mi e po-dobré]

It's OK.

Всичко е наред.
[fsítʃko e naréd]

It's all right.

Всичко е наред.
[fsítʃko e naréd]

At the pharmacy

pharmacy (drugstore)
аптека
[aptéka]

24-hour pharmacy
денонощна аптека
[denonóʃtna aptéka]

Where is the closest pharmacy?
Къде е най-близката аптека?
[kədé e naj-blízkata aptéka?]

Is it open now?
Сега отворена ли е?
[segá otvórena li e?]

At what time does it open?
В колко се отваря?
[v kólko se otvárʲa?]

At what time does it close?
До колко работи?
[do kólko ráboti?]

Is it far?
Далече ли е?
[dalétʃe li e?]

Can I get there on foot?
Ще стигна ли дотам пеша?
[ʃte stígna li dotám péʃa?]

Can you show me on the map?
Покажете ми на картата, моля.
[pokaʒéte mi na kártata, mólʲa]

Please give me something for ...
Дайте ми нещо за ...
[dájte mi néʃto za ...]

a headache
главоболие
[glavobólie]

a cough
кашлица
[káʃlitsa]

a cold
настинка
[nastínka]

the flu
грип
[grip]

a fever
температура
[temperatúra]

a stomach ache
болки в стомаха
[bólki v stomáha]

nausea
повръщане
[povréʃtane]

diarrhea
диария
[diárija]

constipation
запек
[zápek]

pain in the back
болки в гърба
[bólki v gérba]

chest pain	**болки в гърдите** [bólki v gərdíte]
side stitch	**болки отстрани** [bólki otstraní]
abdominal pain	**болки в корема** [bólki v koréma]

pill	**таблетка** [tablétka]
ointment, cream	**маз, мехлем, крем** [maz, mehlém, krem]
syrup	**сироп** [siróp]
spray	**спрей** [sprej]
drops	**капки** [kápki]

You need to go to the hospital.	**Трябва да отидете в болница.** [tr'ábva da otidéte v bólnitsa]
health insurance	**застраховка** [zastrahófka]
prescription	**рецепта** [retsépta]
insect repellant	**препарат от насекоми** [preparát ot nasekómi]
Band Aid	**лейкопласт** [lejkoplást]

The bare minimum

Excuse me, ...	**Извинете, ...**
	[izvinéte, ...]
Hello.	**Здравейте.**
	[zdravéjte]
Thank you.	**Благодаря.**
	[blagodar'á]
Good bye.	**Довиждане.**
	[dovíʒdane]
Yes.	**Да.**
	[da]
No.	**Не.**
	[ne]
I don't know.	**Аз не знам.**
	[az ne znam]
Where? | Where to? | When?	**Къде? | Накъде? | Кога?**
	[kədé? | nakədé? | kogá?]

I need ...	**Трябва ми ...**
	[tr'ábva mi ...]
I want ...	**Аз искам ...**
	[az ískam ...]
Do you have ...?	**Имате ли ...?**
	[ímate li ...?]
Is there a ... here?	**Тук има ли ...?**
	[tuk íma li ...?]
May I ...?	**Мога ли ...?**
	[móga li ...?]
..., please (polite request)	**Моля.**
	[mól'a]

I'm looking for ...	**Аз търся ...**
	[az térs'a ...]
the restroom	**тоалетна**
	[toalétna]
an ATM	**банкомат**
	[bankomát]
a pharmacy (drugstore)	**аптека**
	[aptéka]
a hospital	**болница**
	[bólnitsa]
the police station	**полицейски участък**
	[politséjski uʧástək]
the subway	**метро**
	[metró]

a taxi	**такси**
	[táksi]
the train station	**гара**
	[gára]

My name is …	**Казвам се …**
	[kázvam se …]
What's your name?	**Как се казвате?**
	[kak se kázvate?]
Could you please help me?	**Помогнете ми, моля.**
	[pomognéte mi, mólʲa]
I've got a problem.	**Аз имам проблем.**
	[az ímam problém]
I don't feel well.	**Лошо ми е.**
	[lóʃo mi e]
Call an ambulance!	**Повикайте бърза помощ!**
	[povikájte bǽrza pómoʃt!]
May I make a call?	**Може ли да се обадя?**
	[móʒe li da se obádʲa?]

I'm sorry.	**Извинявам се.**
	[izvinʲávam se]
You're welcome.	**Моля.**
	[mólʲa]

I, me	**аз**
	[az]
you (inform.)	**ти**
	[ti]
he	**той**
	[toj]
she	**тя**
	[tʲa]
they (masc.)	**те**
	[te]
they (fem.)	**те**
	[te]
we	**ние**
	[nie]
you (pl)	**вие**
	[víe]
you (sg, form.)	**Вие**
	[víe]

ENTRANCE	**ВХОД**
	[vhod]
EXIT	**ИЗХОД**
	[íshot]
OUT OF ORDER	**НЕ РАБОТИ**
	[ne ráboti]
CLOSED	**ЗАТВОРЕНО**
	[zatvóreno]

OPEN

ОТВОРЕНО
[otvóreno]

FOR WOMEN

ЗА ЖЕНИ
[za ʒení]

FOR MEN

ЗА МЪЖЕ
[za məʒé]

T&P BOOKS

TOPICAL
VOCABULARY

This section contains more than 3,000 of the most important words.
The dictionary will provide invaluable assistance while traveling abroad, because frequently individual words are enough for you to be understood.
The dictionary includes a convenient transcription of each foreign word

T&P Books Publishing

VOCABULARY
CONTENTS

T&P Books Publishing

BASIC CONCEPTS

T&P Books Publishing

1. Pronouns

I, me	**аз**	[az]
you	**ти**	[ti]
he	**той**	[toj]
she	**тя**	[tʲa]
it	**то**	[to]
we	**ние**	[níe]
you (to a group)	**вие**	[víe]
they	**те**	[te]

2. Greetings. Salutations

Hello! (fam.)	**Здравей!**	[zdravéj]
Hello! (form.)	**Здравейте!**	[zdravéjte]
Good morning!	**Добро утро!**	[dobró útro]
Good afternoon!	**Добър ден!**	[dóbər den]
Good evening!	**Добър вечер!**	[dóbər vétʃer]
to say hello	**поздравявам**	[pozdravʲávam]
Hi! (hello)	**Здрасти!**	[zdrásti]
greeting (n)	**поздрав** (м)	[pózdrav]
to greet (vt)	**приветствувам**	[privétstvuvam]
How are you?	**Как си?**	[kak si]
What's new?	**Какво ново?**	[kakvó nóvo]
Bye-Bye! Goodbye!	**Довиждане!**	[dovíʒdane]
See you soon!	**До скора среща!**	[do skóra sréʃta]
Farewell!	**Сбогом!**	[zbógom]
to say goodbye	**сбогувам се**	[sbogúvam se]
So long!	**До скоро!**	[do skóro]
Thank you!	**Благодаря!**	[blagodarʲá]
Thank you very much!	**Много благодаря!**	[mnógo blagodarʲá]
You're welcome	**Моля.**	[mólʲa]
Don't mention it!	**Няма нищо.**	[nʲáma níʃto]
It was nothing	**Няма за какво.**	[nʲáma za kakvó]
Excuse me! (fam.)	**Извинявай!**	[izvinʲávaj]
Excuse me! (form.)	**Извинявайте!**	[izvinʲávajte]
to excuse (forgive)	**извинявам**	[izvinʲávam]
to apologize (vi)	**извинявам се**	[izvinʲávam se]

My apologies	Моите извинения.	[móite izvinénija]
I'm sorry!	Прощавайте!	[proʃtávajte]
please (adv)	моля	[mólʲa]

Don't forget!	Не забравяйте!	[ne zabrávʲajte]
Certainly!	Разбира се!	[razbíra se]
Of course not!	Разбира се, не!	[razbíra se ne]
Okay! (I agree)	Съгласен!	[səglásen]
That's enough!	Стига!	[stíga]

3. Questions

Who?	Кой?	[koj]
What?	Какво?	[kakvó]
Where? (at, in)	Къде?	[kədé]
Where (to)?	Къде?	[kədé]
From where?	Откъде?	[otkədé]
When?	Кога?	[kogá]
Why? (What for?)	За какво?	[za kakvó]
Why? (~ are you crying?)	Защо?	[zaʃtó]

What for?	За какво?	[za kakvó]
How? (in what way)	Как?	[kak]
Which?	Кой?	[koj]

To whom?	На кого?	[na kogó]
About whom?	За кого?	[za kogó]
About what?	За какво?	[za kakvó]
With whom?	С кого?	[s kogó]
How many? How much?	Колко?	[kólko]
Whose?	Чий?	[tʃij]

4. Prepositions

with (accompanied by)	с ...	[s]
without	без	[bez]
to (indicating direction)	в, във	[v], [vef]
about (talking ~ ...)	за	[za]
before (in time)	преди	[predí]
in front of ...	пред ...	[pret]

under (beneath, below)	под	[pot]
above (over)	над	[nat]
on (atop)	върху	[verhú]
from (off, out of)	от	[ot]
of (made from)	от	[ot]
in (e.g., ~ ten minutes)	след	[slet]
over (across the top of)	през	[pres]

5. Function words. Adverbs. Part 1

Where? (at, in)	**Къде?**	[kədé]
here (adv)	**тук**	[tuk]
there (adv)	**там**	[tam]
somewhere (to be)	**някъде**	[nʲákəde]
nowhere (not in any place)	**никъде**	[níkəde]
by (near, beside)	**до …**	[do]
by the window	**до прозореца**	[do prozóretsa]
Where (to)?	**Къде?**	[kədé]
here (e.g., come ~!)	**тук**	[tuk]
there (e.g., to go ~)	**нататък**	[natátək]
from here (adv)	**оттук**	[ottúk]
from there (adv)	**оттам**	[ottám]
close (adv)	**близо**	[blízo]
far (adv)	**далече**	[dalétʃe]
near (e.g., ~ Paris)	**до**	[do]
nearby (adv)	**редом**	[rédom]
not far (adv)	**недалече**	[nedalétʃe]
left (adj)	**ляв**	[lʲav]
on the left	**отляво**	[otlʲávo]
to the left	**вляво**	[vlʲávo]
right (adj)	**десен**	[désen]
on the right	**отдясно**	[otdʲásno]
to the right	**вдясно**	[vdʲásno]
in front (adv)	**отпред**	[otprét]
front (as adj)	**преден**	[préden]
ahead (the kids ran ~)	**напред**	[naprét]
behind (adv)	**отзад**	[otzát]
from behind	**отзад**	[otzát]
back (towards the rear)	**назад**	[nazát]
middle	**среда** (ж)	[sredá]
in the middle	**по средата**	[po sredáta]
at the side	**встрани**	[fstraní]
everywhere (adv)	**навсякъде**	[nafsʲákəde]
around (in all directions)	**наоколо**	[naókolo]
from inside	**отвътре**	[otvétre]
somewhere (to go)	**някъде**	[nʲákəde]
straight (directly)	**направо**	[naprávo]

back (e.g., come ~)	обратно	[obrátno]
from anywhere	откъдето и да е	[otkədéto i da e]
from somewhere	отнякъде	[otnʲákəde]

firstly (adv)	първо	[pэ́rvo]
secondly (adv)	второ	[ftóro]
thirdly (adv)	трето	[tréto]

suddenly (adv)	изведнъж	[izvednэ́ʃ]
at first (in the beginning)	в началото	[f natʃáloto]
for the first time	за пръв път	[za prəv pэ́t]
long before ...	много време преди ...	[mnógo vréme predí]
anew (over again)	наново	[nanóvo]
for good (adv)	завинаги	[zavínagi]

never (adv)	никога	[níkoga]
again (adv)	пак	[pak]
now (at present)	сега	[segá]
often (adv)	често	[tʃésto]
then (adv)	тогава	[togáva]
urgently (quickly)	срочно	[sróʧno]
usually (adv)	обикновено	[obiknovéno]

by the way, ...	между другото ...	[méʒdu drúgoto]
possibly	възможно	[vəzmóʒno]
probably (adv)	вероятно	[verojátno]
maybe (adv)	може би	[móʒe bi]
besides ...	освен това, ...	[osvén tová]
that's why ...	затова	[zatová]
in spite of ...	въпреки че ...	[vэ́preki ʧe]
thanks to ...	благодарение на ...	[blagodarénie na]

what (pron.)	какво	[kakvó]
that (conj.)	че	[ʧe]
something	нещо	[néʃto]

anything (something)	нещо	[néʃto]
nothing	нищо	[níʃto]

who (pron.)	кой	[koj]
someone	някой	[nʲákoj]
somebody	някой	[nʲákoj]

nobody	никой	[níkoj]
nowhere (a voyage to ~)	никъде	[níkəde]

nobody's	ничий	[nítʃij]
somebody's	нечий	[nétʃij]

so (I'm ~ glad)	така	[taká]
also (as well)	също така	[sэ́ʃto taká]
too (as well)	също	[sэ́ʃto]

6. Function words. Adverbs. Part 2

Why?	Защо?	[zaʃtó]
for some reason	кой знае защо	[koj znáe zaʃtó]
because ...	защото ...	[zaʃtóto]
for some purpose	кой знае защо	[koj znáe zaʃtó]

and	и	[i]
or	или	[ilí]
but	но	[no]
for (e.g., ~ me)	за	[za]

too (~ many people)	прекалено	[prekaléno]
only (exclusively)	само	[sámo]
exactly (adv)	точно	[tótʃno]
about (more or less)	около	[ókolo]

approximately (adv)	приблизително	[pribliзítelno]
approximate (adj)	приблизителен	[pribliзítelen]
almost (adv)	почти	[potʃtí]
the rest	остатък (м)	[ostátək]

the other (second)	друг	[druk]
other (different)	друг	[druk]
each (adj)	всеки	[fséki]
any (no matter which)	всеки	[fséki]
many, much (a lot of)	много	[mnógo]
many people	много	[mnógo]
all (everyone)	всички	[fsítʃki]

in return for ...	в обмяна на ...	[v obmʲána na]
in exchange (adv)	в замяна	[v zamʲána]
by hand (made)	ръчно	[rátʃno]
hardly (negative opinion)	едва ли	[edvá li]

probably (adv)	вероятно	[verojátno]
on purpose (intentionally)	специално	[spetsiálno]
by accident (adv)	случайно	[slutʃájno]

very (adv)	много	[mnógo]
for example (adv)	например	[naprímer]
between	между	[meзdú]
among	сред	[sret]
so much (such a lot)	толкова	[tólkova]
especially (adv)	особено	[osóbeno]

NUMBERS.
MISCELLANEOUS

T&P Books Publishing

0 zero	нула (ж)	[núla]
1 one	едно	[ednó]
2 two	две	[dve]
3 three	три	[tri]
4 four	четири	[ʧétiri]
5 five	пет	[pet]
6 six	шест	[ʃest]
7 seven	седем	[sédem]
8 eight	осем	[ósem]
9 nine	девет	[dévet]
10 ten	десет	[déset]
11 eleven	единадесет	[edinádeset]
12 twelve	дванадесет	[dvanádeset]
13 thirteen	тринадесет	[trinádeset]
14 fourteen	четиринадесет	[ʧetirinádeset]
15 fifteen	петнадесет	[petnádeset]
16 sixteen	шестнадесет	[ʃesnádeset]
17 seventeen	седемнадесет	[sedemnádeset]
18 eighteen	осемнадесет	[osemnádeset]
19 nineteen	деветнадесет	[devetnádeset]
20 twenty	двадесет	[dvádeset]
21 twenty-one	двадесет и едно	[dvádeset i ednó]
22 twenty-two	двадесет и две	[dvádeset i dve]
23 twenty-three	двадесет и три	[dvádeset i tri]
30 thirty	тридесет	[trídeset]
31 thirty-one	тридесет и едно	[trídeset i ednó]
32 thirty-two	тридесет и две	[trídeset i dve]
33 thirty-three	тридесет и три	[trídeset i tri]
40 forty	четиридесет	[ʧetírideset]
41 forty-one	четиридесет и едно	[ʧetírideset i ednó]
42 forty-two	четиридесет и две	[ʧetírideset i dve]
43 forty-three	четиридесет и три	[ʧetírideset i tri]
50 fifty	петдесет	[petdesét]
51 fifty-one	петдесет и едно	[petdesét i ednó]
52 fifty-two	петдесет и две	[petdesét i dve]
53 fifty-three	петдесет и три	[petdesét i tri]
60 sixty	шестдесет	[ʃestdesét]

61 sixty-one	шестдесет и едно	[ʃestdesét i ednó]
62 sixty-two	шестдесет и две	[ʃestdesét i dve]
63 sixty-three	шестдесет и три	[ʃestesét i tri]

70 seventy	седемдесет	[sedemdesét]
71 seventy-one	седемдесет и едно	[sedemdesét i ednó]
72 seventy-two	седемдесет и две	[sedemdesét i dve]
73 seventy-three	седемдесет и три	[sedemdesét i tri]

80 eighty	осемдесет	[osemdesét]
81 eighty-one	осемдесет и едно	[osemdesét i ednó]
82 eighty-two	осемдесет и две	[osemdesét i dve]
83 eighty-three	осемдесет и три	[osemdesét i tri]

90 ninety	деветдесет	[devetdesét]
91 ninety-one	деветдесет и едно	[devetdesét i ednó]
92 ninety-two	деветдесет и две	[devetdesét i dve]
93 ninety-three	деветдесет и три	[devetdesét i tri]

8. Cardinal numbers. Part 2

100 one hundred	сто	[sto]
200 two hundred	двеста	[dvésta]
300 three hundred	триста	[trísta]
400 four hundred	четиристотин	[tʃétiri·stótin]
500 five hundred	петстотин	[pét·stótin]

600 six hundred	шестстотин	[ʃést·stótin]
700 seven hundred	седемстотин	[sédem·stótin]
800 eight hundred	осемстотин	[ósem·stótin]
900 nine hundred	деветстотин	[dévet·stótin]

1000 one thousand	хиляда (ж)	[hilʲáda]
2000 two thousand	две хиляди	[dve hílʲadi]
3000 three thousand	три хиляди	[tri hílʲadi]
10000 ten thousand	десет хиляди	[déset hílʲadi]
one hundred thousand	сто хиляди	[sto hílʲadi]
million	милион (м)	[milión]
billion	милиард (м)	[miliárt]

9. Ordinal numbers

first (adj)	първи	[pérvi]
second (adj)	втори	[ftóri]
third (adj)	трети	[tréti]
fourth (adj)	четвърти	[tʃetvérti]
fifth (adj)	пети	[péti]
sixth (adj)	шести	[ʃésti]

seventh (adj)	**седми**	[sédmi]
eighth (adj)	**осми**	[ósmi]
ninth (adj)	**девети**	[devéti]
tenth (adj)	**десети**	[deséti]

COLOURS. UNITS OF MEASUREMENT

T&P Books Publishing

10. Colors

color	цвят (м)	[tsvʲat]
shade (tint)	оттенък (м)	[otténək]
hue	тон (м)	[ton]
rainbow	небесна дъга (ж)	[nebésna dəgá]
white (adj)	бял	[bʲal]
black (adj)	черен	[ʧéren]
gray (adj)	сив	[siv]
green (adj)	зелен	[zelén]
yellow (adj)	жълт	[ʒəlt]
red (adj)	червен	[ʧervén]
blue (adj)	син	[sin]
light blue (adj)	небесносин	[nebesnosín]
pink (adj)	розов	[rózov]
orange (adj)	оранжев	[oránʒev]
violet (adj)	виолетов	[violétov]
brown (adj)	кафяв	[kafʲáv]
golden (adj)	златен	[zláten]
silvery (adj)	сребрист	[srebríst]
beige (adj)	бежов	[béʒov]
cream (adj)	кремав	[krémaf]
turquoise (adj)	тюркоазен	[tʲurkoázen]
cherry red (adj)	вишнев	[víʃnev]
lilac (adj)	лилав	[liláf]
crimson (adj)	малинов	[malínov]
light (adj)	светъл	[svétəl]
dark (adj)	тъмен	[témen]
bright, vivid (adj)	ярък	[járək]
colored (pencils)	цветен	[tsvéten]
color (e.g., ~ film)	цветен	[tsvéten]
black-and-white (adj)	черно-бял	[ʧérno-bʲal]
plain (one-colored)	едноцветен	[edno·tsvéten]
multicolored (adj)	многоцветен	[mnogo·tsvéten]

11. Units of measurement

weight	тегло (с)	[tegló]
length	дължина (ж)	[dəʤiná]

width	широчина (ж)	[ʃirotʃiná]
height	височина (ж)	[visotʃiná]
depth	дълбочина (ж)	[dəlbotʃiná]
volume	обем (м)	[obém]
area	площ (ж)	[ploʃt]

gram	грам (м)	[gram]
milligram	милиграм (м)	[miligrám]
kilogram	килограм (м)	[kilográm]
ton	тон (м)	[ton]
pound	фунт (м)	[funt]
ounce	унция (ж)	[úntsija]

meter	метър (м)	[métər]
millimeter	милиметър (м)	[milimétər]
centimeter	сантиметър (м)	[santimétər]
kilometer	километър (м)	[kilométər]
mile	миля (ж)	[mílʲa]

inch	дюйм (м)	[dʲujm]
foot	фут (м)	[fut]
yard	ярд (м)	[jart]

square meter	квадратен метър (м)	[kvadráten métər]
hectare	хектар (м)	[hektár]
liter	литър (м)	[lítər]
degree	градус (м)	[grádus]
volt	волт (м)	[volt]
ampere	ампер (м)	[ampér]
horsepower	конска сила (ж)	[kónska síla]

quantity	количество (ц)	[kolítʃestvo]
a little bit of ...	малко ...	[málko]
half	половина (ж)	[polovína]
dozen	дузина (ж)	[duzína]
piece (item)	брой (м)	[broj]

| size | размер (м) | [razmér] |
| scale (map ~) | мащаб (м) | [maʃtáp] |

minimal (adj)	минимален	[minimálen]
the smallest (adj)	най-малък	[naj-málək]
medium (adj)	среден	[sréden]
maximal (adj)	максимален	[maksimálen]
the largest (adj)	най-голям	[naj-golʲám]

12. Containers

| canning jar (glass ~) | буркан (м) | [burkán] |
| can | тенекия (ж) | [tenekíja] |

bucket	кофа (ж)	[kófa]
barrel	бъчва (ж)	[bə́tʃva]
wash basin (e.g., plastic ~)	леген (м)	[legén]
tank (100L water ~)	резервоар (м)	[rezervoár]
hip flask	манерка (ж)	[manérka]
jerrycan	туба (ж)	[túba]
tank (e.g., tank car)	цистерна (ж)	[tsistérna]
mug	чаша (ж)	[tʃáʃa]
cup (of coffee, etc.)	чаша (ж)	[tʃáʃa]
saucer	чинийка (ж)	[tʃiníjka]
glass (tumbler)	стакан (м)	[stakán]
wine glass	чаша (ж) за вино	[tʃáʃa za víno]
stock pot (soup pot)	тенджера (ж)	[téndʒera]
bottle (~ of wine)	бутилка (ж)	[butílka]
neck (of the bottle, etc.)	гърло (с) на бутилка	[gə́rlo na butílka]
carafe (decanter)	гарафа (ж)	[garáfa]
pitcher	кана (ж)	[kána]
vessel (container)	съд (м)	[sət]
pot (crock, stoneware ~)	гърне (с)	[gərné]
vase	ваза (ж)	[váza]
flacon, bottle (perfume ~)	шишенце (с)	[ʃiʃéntse]
vial, small bottle	шишенце (с)	[ʃiʃéntse]
tube (of toothpaste)	тубичка (ж)	[túbitʃka]
sack (bag)	чувал (м)	[tʃuvál]
bag (paper ~, plastic ~)	плик (м)	[plik]
pack (of cigarettes, etc.)	кутия (ж)	[kutíja]
box (e.g., shoebox)	кутия (ж)	[kutíja]
crate	щайга (ж)	[ʃtájga]
basket	кошница (ж)	[kóʃnitsa]

BOOKS

MAIN VERBS

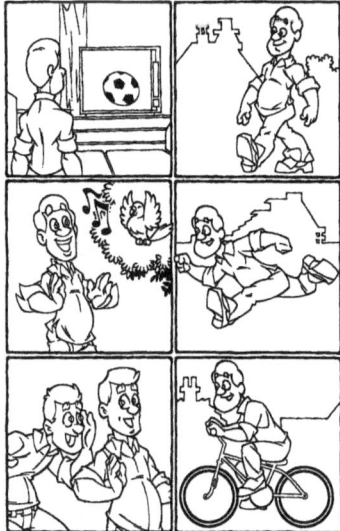

T&P Books Publishing

to advise (vt)	съветвам	[səvétvam]
to agree (say yes)	съгласявам се	[səglasʲávam se]
to answer (vi, vt)	отговарям	[otgovárʲam]
to arrive (vi)	пристигам	[pristígam]

to ask (~ oneself)	питам	[pítam]
to ask (~ sb to do sth)	моля	[mólʲa]
to be (vi)	съм, бъда	[səm], [béda]

to be afraid	страхувам се	[strahúvam se]
to be hungry	искам да ям	[ískam da jam]
to be interested in …	интересувам се	[interesúvam se]

| to be needed | трябвам | [trʲábvam] |
| to be surprised | удивлявам се | [udivlʲávam se] |

to be thirsty	искам да пия	[ískam da píja]
to begin (vt)	започвам	[zapóʧvam]
to belong to …	принадлежа …	[prinadleʒá]

| to boast (vi) | хваля се | [hválʲa se] |
| to break (split into pieces) | чупя | [ʧúpʲa] |

to call (~ for help)	викам	[víkam]
can (v aux)	мога	[móga]
to catch (vt)	ловя	[lovʲá]

| to change (vt) | сменям | [sménʲam] |
| to choose (select) | избирам | [izbíram] |

to come down (the stairs)	слизам	[slízam]
to compare (vt)	сравнявам	[sravnʲávam]
to complain (vi, vt)	оплаквам се	[oplákvam se]
to confuse (mix up)	обърквам	[obérkvam]

| to continue (vt) | продължавам | [prodəlʒávam] |
| to control (vt) | контролирам | [kontrolíram] |

to cook (dinner)	готвя	[gótvʲa]
to cost (vt)	струвам	[strúvam]
to count (add up)	броя	[brojá]
to count on …	разчитам на …	[rasʧítam na]
to create (vt)	създам	[səzdám]
to cry (weep)	плача	[pláʧa]

14. The most important verbs. Part 2

to deceive (vi, vt)	лъжа	[léʒa]
to decorate (tree, street)	украсявам	[ukrasʲávam]
to defend (a country, etc.)	защитавам	[zaʃtitávam]
to demand (request firmly)	изисквам	[izískvam]
to dig (vt)	ровя	[róvʲa]

to discuss (vt)	обсъждам	[obséʒdam]
to do (vt)	правя	[právʲa]
to doubt (have doubts)	съмнявам се	[səmnʲávam se]
to drop (let fall)	изтървавам	[istərvávam]
to enter	влизам	[vlízam]
(room, house, etc.)		

to excuse (forgive)	извинявам	[izvinʲávam]
to exist (vi)	съществувам	[səʃtestvúvam]
to expect (foresee)	предвиждам	[predvíʒdam]

to explain (vt)	обяснявам	[obʲasnʲávam]
to fall (vi)	падам	[pádam]

to find (vt)	намирам	[namíram]
to finish (vt)	приключвам	[priklʲútʃvam]
to fly (vi)	летя	[letʲá]

to follow ... (come after)	вървя след ...	[varvʲá slet]
to forget (vi, vt)	забравям	[zabrávʲam]

to forgive (vt)	прощавам	[proʃtávam]
to give (vt)	давам	[dávam]

to give a hint	намеквам	[namékvam]
to go (on foot)	вървя	[vərvʲá]

to go for a swim	къпя се	[képʲa se]
to go out (for dinner, etc.)	излизам	[izlízam]
to guess (the answer)	отгатна	[otgátna]

to have (vt)	имам	[ímam]
to have breakfast	закусвам	[zakúsvam]
to have dinner	вечерям	[vetʃérʲam]

to have lunch	обядвам	[obʲádvam]
to hear (vt)	чувам	[tʃúvam]

to help (vt)	помагам	[pomágam]
to hide (vt)	крия	[kríja]
to hope (vi, vt)	надявам се	[nadʲávam se]
to hunt (vi, vt)	ловувам	[lovúvam]
to hurry (vi)	бързам	[bérzam]

15. The most important verbs. Part 3

to inform (vt)	информирам	[informíram]
to insist (vi, vt)	настоявам	[nastojávam]
to insult (vt)	оскърбявам	[oskərbʲávam]
to invite (vt)	каня	[kánʲa]
to joke (vi)	шегувам се	[ʃegúvam se]
to keep (vt)	съхранявам	[səhranʲávam]
to keep silent, to hush	мълча	[məltʃá]
to kill (vt)	убивам	[ubívam]
to know (sb)	познавам	[poznávam]
to know (sth)	знам	[znam]
to laugh (vi)	смея се	[sméja se]
to liberate (city, etc.)	освобождавам	[osvoboʒdávam]
to like (I like …)	харесвам	[harésvam]
to look for … (search)	търся	[tə́rsʲa]
to love (sb)	обичам	[obítʃam]
to make a mistake	греша	[greʃá]
to manage, to run	ръководя	[rəkovódʲa]
to mean (signify)	означавам	[oznatʃávam]
to mention (talk about)	споменавам	[spomenávam]
to miss (school, etc.)	пропускам	[propúskam]
to notice (see)	забелязвам	[zabelʲázvam]
to object (vi, vt)	възразявам	[vəzrazʲávam]
to observe (see)	наблюдавам	[nablʲudávam]
to open (vt)	отварям	[otvárʲam]
to order (meal, etc.)	поръчвам	[porə́tʃvam]
to order (mil.)	заповядвам	[zapovʲádvam]
to own (possess)	владея	[vladéja]
to participate (vi)	участвам	[utʃástvam]
to pay (vi, vt)	плащам	[pláʃtam]
to permit (vt)	разрешавам	[razreʃávam]
to plan (vt)	планирам	[planíram]
to play (children)	играя	[igrája]
to pray (vi, vt)	моля се	[mólʲa se]
to prefer (vt)	предпочитам	[pretpotʃítam]
to promise (vt)	обещавам	[obeʃtávam]
to pronounce (vt)	произнасям	[proiznásʲam]
to propose (vt)	предлагам	[predlágam]
to punish (vt)	наказвам	[nakázvam]

16. The most important verbs. Part 4

to read (vi, vt)	чета	[tʃeta]
to recommend (vt)	съветвам	[səvétvam]

to refuse (vi, vt)	отказвам се	[otkázvam se]
to regret (be sorry)	съжалявам	[seʒalʲávam]
to rent (sth from sb)	наемам	[naémam]

to repeat (say again)	повтарям	[poftárʲam]
to reserve, to book	резервирам	[rezervíram]
to run (vi)	бягам	[bʲágam]
to save (rescue)	спасявам	[spasʲávam]
to say (~ thank you)	кажа	[káʒa]

to scold (vt)	ругая	[rugája]
to see (vt)	виждам	[víʒdam]
to sell (vt)	продавам	[prodávam]
to send (vt)	изпращам	[ispráʃtam]
to shoot (vi)	стрелям	[strélʲam]

to shout (vi)	викам	[víkam]
to show (vt)	показвам	[pokázvam]
to sign (document)	подписвам	[potpísvam]
to sit down (vi)	сядам	[sʲádam]

to smile (vi)	усмихвам се	[usmíhvam se]
to speak (vi, vt)	говоря	[govórʲa]
to steal (money, etc.)	крада	[kradá]
to stop (for pause, etc.)	спирам се	[spíram se]
to stop (please ~ calling me)	прекратявам	[prekratʲávam]

to study (vt)	изучавам	[izutʃávam]
to swim (vi)	плувам	[plúvam]
to take (vt)	взимам	[vzímam]
to think (vi, vt)	мисля	[mislʲa]
to threaten (vt)	заплашвам	[zapláʃvam]

to touch (with hands)	пипам	[pípam]
to translate (vt)	превеждам	[prevéʒdam]
to trust (vt)	доверявам	[doverʲávam]
to try (attempt)	опитвам се	[opítvam se]
to turn (e.g., ~ left)	завивам	[zavívam]

to underestimate (vt)	недооценявам	[nedootsenʲávam]
to understand (vt)	разбирам	[razbíram]
to unite (vt)	обединявам	[obedinʲávam]
to wait (vt)	чакам	[tʃákam]

to want (wish, desire)	искам	[ískam]
to warn (vt)	предупреждавам	[predupreʒdávam]
to work (vi)	работя	[rabótʲa]
to write (vt)	пиша	[píʃa]
to write down	записвам	[zapísvam]

BOOKS

T&P

TIME. CALENDAR

T&P Books Publishing

17. Weekdays

Monday	понеделник (м)	[ponedélnik]
Tuesday	вторник (м)	[ftórnik]
Wednesday	сряда (ж)	[srʲáda]
Thursday	четвъртък (м)	[ʧetvártək]
Friday	петък (м)	[pétək]
Saturday	събота (ж)	[sébota]
Sunday	неделя (ж)	[nedélʲa]

today (adv)	днес	[dnes]
tomorrow (adv)	утре	[útre]
the day after tomorrow	вдругиден	[vdrugidén]
yesterday (adv)	вчера	[vʧéra]
the day before yesterday	завчера	[závʧera]

day	ден (м)	[den]
working day	работен ден (м)	[rabóten den]
public holiday	празничен ден (м)	[práznitʃen den]
day off	почивен ден (м)	[potʃíven dén]
weekend	почивни дни (м мн)	[potʃívni dni]

all day long	цял ден	[tsʲal den]
the next day (adv)	на следващия ден	[na slédvaʃtija den]
two days ago	преди два дена	[predí dva déna]
the day before	в навечерието	[v navetʃérieto]
daily (adj)	всекидневен	[fsekidnéven]
every day (adv)	всекидневно	[fsekidnévno]

week	седмица (ж)	[sédmitsa]
last week (adv)	през миналата седмица	[pres mínalata sédmitsa]
next week (adv)	през следващата седмица	[pres slédvaʃtata sédmitsa]
weekly (adj)	седмичен	[sédmitʃen]
every week (adv)	седмично	[sédmitʃno]
twice a week	два пъти на седмица	[dva pətí na sédmitsa]
every Tuesday	всеки вторник	[fséki ftórnik]

18. Hours. Day and night

morning	сутрин (ж)	[sútrin]
in the morning	сутринта	[sutrintá]
noon, midday	пладне (с)	[pládne]
in the afternoon	следобед	[sledóbet]

evening	вечер (ж)	[vétʃer]
in the evening	вечер	[vétʃer]
night	нощ (ж)	[noʃt]
at night	нощем	[nóʃtem]
midnight	полунощ (ж)	[polunóʃt]

second	секунда (ж)	[sekúnda]
minute	минута (ж)	[minúta]
hour	час (м)	[tʃas]
half an hour	половин час (м)	[polovín tʃas]
a quarter-hour	четвърт (ж) час	[tʃétvərt tʃas]
fifteen minutes	петнадесет минути	[petnádeset minúti]
24 hours	денонощие (с)	[denonóʃtie]

sunrise	изгрев слънце (с)	[ízgrev sléntsə]
dawn	разсъмване (с)	[rassémvane]
early morning	ранна сутрин (ж)	[ránna sútrin]
sunset	залез (м)	[zález]

early in the morning	рано сутрин	[ráno sútrin]
this morning	тази сутрин	[tázi sútrin]
tomorrow morning	утре сутрин	[útre sútrin]

this afternoon	днес през деня	[dnes pres denʲá]
in the afternoon	следобед	[sledóbet]
tomorrow afternoon	утре следобед	[útre sledóbet]

| tonight (this evening) | довечера | [dovétʃera] |
| tomorrow night | утре вечер | [útre vétʃer] |

at 3 o'clock sharp	точно в три часа	[tótʃno v tri tʃasá]
about 4 o'clock	около четири часа	[ókolo tʃétiri tʃasá]
by 12 o'clock	към дванадесет часа	[kəm dvanádeset tʃasá]

in 20 minutes	след двадесет минути	[slet dvádeset minúti]
in an hour	след един час	[slet edín tʃas]
on time (adv)	навреме	[navréme]

a quarter to ...	без четвърт ...	[bes tʃétvərt]
within an hour	в течение на един час	[v tetʃénie na edín tʃas]
every 15 minutes	на всеки петнадесет минути	[na fséki petnádeset minúti]

| round the clock | цяло денонощие | [tsʲálo denonóʃtie] |

19. Months. Seasons

January	януари (м)	[januári]
February	февруари (м)	[fevruári]
March	март (м)	[mart]
April	април (м)	[apríl]

May	**май** (м)	[maj]
June	**юни** (м)	[júni]
July	**юли** (м)	[júli]
August	**август** (м)	[ávgust]
September	**септември** (м)	[septémvri]
October	**октомври** (м)	[októmvri]
November	**ноември** (м)	[noémvri]
December	**декември** (м)	[dekémvri]
spring	**пролет** (ж)	[prólet]
in spring	**през пролетта**	[prez prolettá]
spring (as adj)	**пролетен**	[próleten]
summer	**лято** (с)	[lʲáto]
in summer	**през лятото**	[prez lʲátoto]
summer (as adj)	**летен**	[léten]
fall	**есен** (ж)	[ésen]
in fall	**през есента**	[prez esentá]
fall (as adj)	**есенен**	[ésenen]
winter	**зима** (ж)	[zíma]
in winter	**през зимата**	[prez zímata]
winter (as adj)	**зимен**	[zímen]
month	**месец** (м)	[mésets]
this month	**през този месец**	[pres tózi mésets]
next month	**през следващия месец**	[prez slédvaʃtija mésets]
last month	**през миналия месец**	[prez mínalija mésets]
a month ago	**преди един месец**	[predí edín mésets]
in a month (a month later)	**след един месец**	[slet edín mésets]
in 2 months (2 months later)	**след два месеца**	[slet dva mésetsa]
the whole month	**цял месец**	[tsʲal mésets]
all month long	**цял месец**	[tsʲal mésets]
monthly (~ magazine)	**месечен**	[mésetʃen]
monthly (adv)	**месечно**	[mésetʃno]
every month	**всеки месец**	[fséki mésets]
twice a month	**два пъти на месец**	[dva péti na mésets]
year	**година** (ж)	[godína]
this year	**тази година**	[tázi godína]
next year	**през следващата година**	[prez slédvaʃtata godína]
last year	**през миналата година**	[prez mínalata godína]
a year ago	**преди една година**	[predí edná godína]
in a year	**след една година**	[slet edná godína]
in two years	**след две години**	[slet dve godíni]

| the whole year | цяла година | [tsʲála godína] |
| all year long | цяла година | [tsʲála godína] |

every year	всяка година	[fsʲáka godína]
annual (adj)	ежегоден	[eʒegóden]
annually (adv)	ежегодно	[eʒegódno]
4 times a year	четири пъти годишно	[tʃétiri péti godíʃno]

date (e.g., today's ~)	число (с)	[tʃisló]
date (e.g., ~ of birth)	дата (ж)	[dáta]
calendar	календар (м)	[kalendár]

half a year	половин година	[polovín godína]
six months	полугодие (с)	[polugódie]
season (summer, etc.)	сезон (м)	[sezón]
century	век (м)	[vek]

TRAVEL. HOTEL

T&P Books Publishing

20. Trip. Travel

tourism, travel	**туризъм** (м)	[turízəm]
tourist	**турист** (м)	[turíst]
trip, voyage	**пътешествие** (с)	[pəteʃéstvie]
adventure	**приключение** (с)	[priklʲutʃénie]
trip, journey	**пътуване** (с)	[pətúvane]
vacation	**отпуска** (ж)	[ótpuska]
to be on vacation	**бъда в отпуска**	[bə́da v ótpuska]
rest	**почивка** (ж)	[potʃífka]
train	**влак** (м)	[vlak]
by train	**с влак**	[s vlak]
airplane	**самолет** (м)	[samolét]
by airplane	**със самолет**	[səs samolét]
by car	**с кола**	[s kolá]
by ship	**с кораб**	[s kórap]
luggage	**багаж** (м)	[bagáʃ]
suitcase	**куфар** (м)	[kúfar]
luggage cart	**количка** (ж) **за багаж**	[kolítʃka za bagáʃ]
passport	**паспорт** (м)	[paspórt]
visa	**виза** (ж)	[víza]
ticket	**билет** (м)	[bilét]
air ticket	**самолетен билет** (м)	[samoléten bilét]
guidebook	**пътеводител** (м)	[pətevodítel]
map (tourist ~)	**карта** (ж)	[kárta]
area (rural ~)	**местност** (ж)	[méstnost]
place, site	**място** (с)	[mʲásto]
exotica (n)	**екзотика** (ж)	[ekzótika]
exotic (adj)	**екзотичен**	[ekzotítʃen]
amazing (adj)	**удивителен**	[udivítelen]
group	**група** (ж)	[grúpa]
excursion, sightseeing tour	**екскурзия** (ж)	[ekskúrzija]
guide (person)	**гид** (м)	[git]

21. Hotel

hotel	**хотел** (м)	[hotél]
motel	**мотел** (м)	[motél]

three-star (~ hotel)	три звезди	[tri zvezdí]
five-star	пет звезди	[pet zvezdí]
to stay (in a hotel, etc.)	отсядам	[otsʲádam]

room	стая (ж) в хотел	[stája f hotél]
single room	еднинична стая (ж)	[edinítʃna stája]
double room	двойна стая (ж)	[dvójna stája]
to book a room	резервирам стая	[rezervíram stája]

| half board | полупансион (м) | [polupansión] |
| full board | пълен пансион (м) | [pélen pansión] |

with bath	с баня	[s bánʲa]
with shower	с душ	[s duʃ]
satellite television	сателитна телевизия (ж)	[satelítna televízija]
air-conditioner	климатик (м)	[klimatík]
towel	кърпа (ж)	[kérpa]
key	ключ (м)	[klʲutʃ]

administrator	администратор (м)	[administrátor]
chambermaid	камериерка (ж)	[kameriérka]
porter, bellboy	носач (м)	[nosátʃ]
doorman	портиер (м)	[portiér]

restaurant	ресторант (м)	[restoránt]
pub, bar	бар (м)	[bar]
breakfast	закуска (ж)	[zakúska]
dinner	вечеря (ж)	[vetʃérʲa]
buffet	шведска маса (ж)	[ʃvétska mása]

| lobby | вестибюл (м) | [vestibʲúl] |
| elevator | асансьор (м) | [asansʲór] |

| DO NOT DISTURB | НЕ МЕ БЕЗПОКОЙТЕ! | [ne me bespokójte] |
| NO SMOKING | ПУШЕНЕТО ЗАБРАНЕНО! | [puʃenéto zabráneno] |

22. Sightseeing

monument	паметник (м)	[pámetnik]
fortress	крепост (ж)	[krépost]
palace	дворец (м)	[dvoréts]
castle	замък (м)	[zámək]
tower	кула (ж)	[kúla]
mausoleum	мавзолей (м)	[mavzoléj]

architecture	архитектура (ж)	[arhitektúra]
medieval (adj)	средновековен	[srednovekóven]
ancient (adj)	старинен	[starínen]
national (adj)	национален	[natsionálen]

famous (monument, etc.)	**известен**	[izvésten]
tourist	**турист** (м)	[turíst]
guide (person)	**гид** (м)	[git]
excursion, sightseeing tour	**екскурзия** (ж)	[ekskúrzija]
to show (vt)	**показвам**	[pokázvam]
to tell (vt)	**разказвам**	[raskázvam]
to find (vt)	**намеря**	[namérʲa]
to get lost (lose one's way)	**загубя се**	[zagúbʲa se]
map (e.g., subway ~)	**схема** (ж)	[shéma]
map (e.g., city ~)	**план** (м)	[plan]
souvenir, gift	**сувенир** (м)	[suvenír]
gift shop	**сувенирен магазин** (м)	[suveníren magazín]
to take pictures	**снимам**	[snímam]
to have one's picture taken	**снимам се**	[snímam se]

T&P BOOKS

TRANSPORTATION

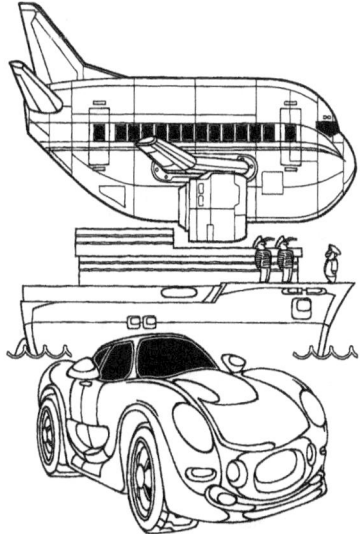

T&P Books Publishing

airport	**летище** (с)	[letíʃte]
airplane	**самолет** (м)	[samolét]
airline	**авиокомпания** (ж)	[aviokompánija]
air traffic controller	**авиодиспечер** (м)	[aviodispétʃer]
departure	**излитане** (с)	[izlítane]
arrival	**кацане** (с)	[kátsane]
to arrive (by plane)	**кацна**	[kátsna]
departure time	**време** (с) **на излитане**	[vréme na izlítane]
arrival time	**време** (с) **на кацане**	[vréme na kátsane]
to be delayed	**закъснявам**	[zakəsnʲávam]
flight delay	**закъснение** (с) **на излитане**	[zakəsnénie na izlítane]
information board	**информационно табло** (с)	[informatsiónno tabló]
information	**информация** (ж)	[informátsija]
to announce (vt)	**обявявам**	[obʲavʲávam]
flight (e.g., next ~)	**рейс** (м)	[rejs]
customs	**митница** (ж)	[mítnitsa]
customs officer	**митничар** (м)	[mitnitʃár]
customs declaration	**декларация** (ж)	[deklarátsija]
to fill out (vt)	**попълня**	[popélnʲa]
to fill out the declaration	**попълня декларация**	[popélnʲa deklarátsija]
passport control	**паспортен контрол** (м)	[paspórten kontról]
luggage	**багаж** (м)	[bagáʃ]
hand luggage	**ръчен багаж** (м)	[rátʃen bagáʃ]
luggage cart	**количка** (ж)	[kolítʃka]
landing	**кацане** (с)	[kátsane]
landing strip	**писта** (ж) **за кацане**	[písta za kátsane]
to land (vi)	**кацам**	[kátsam]
airstair (passenger stair)	**стълба** (ж)	[stélba]
check-in	**регистрация** (ж)	[registrátsija]
check-in counter	**гише** (с) **за регистрация**	[giʃé za registrátsija]
to check-in (vi)	**регистрирам се**	[registríram se]
boarding pass	**бордна карта** (ж)	[bórdna kárta]
departure gate	**излизане** (с)	[izlízane]

transit	транзит (м)	[tranzít]
to wait (vt)	чакам	[ʧákam]
departure lounge	чакалня (ж)	[ʧakálnʲa]
to see off	изпращам	[ispráʃtam]
to say goodbye	сбогувам се	[sbogúvam se]

24. Airplane

airplane	самолет (м)	[samolét]
air ticket	самолетен билет (м)	[samoléten bilét]
airline	авиокомпания (ж)	[aviokompánija]
airport	летище (с)	[letíʃte]
supersonic (adj)	свръхзвуков	[svrəh·zvúkov]

captain	командир (м) на самолет	[komandír na samolét]
crew	екипаж (м)	[ekipáʒ]
pilot	пилот (м)	[pilót]
flight attendant (fem.)	стюардеса (ж)	[stʲuardésa]
navigator	щурман (м)	[ʃtúrman]

wings	крила (мн)	[krilá]
tail	опашка (ж)	[opáʃka]
cockpit	кабина (ж)	[kabína]
engine	двигател (м)	[dvigátel]
undercarriage (landing gear)	шаси (мн)	[ʃasí]
turbine	турбина (ж)	[turbína]

propeller	перка (ж)	[perka]
black box	черна кутия (ж)	[ʧérna kutíja]
yoke (control column)	кормило (с)	[kormílo]
fuel	гориво (с)	[gorívo]

safety card	инструкция (ж)	[instrúktsija]
oxygen mask	кислородна маска (ж)	[kisloródna máska]
uniform	униформа (ж)	[unifórma]
life vest	спасителна жилетка (ж)	[spasítelna ʒilétka]
parachute	парашут (м)	[paraʃút]

takeoff	излитане (с)	[izlítane]
to take off (vi)	излитам	[izlítam]
runway	писта (ж) за излитане	[písta za izlítane]

visibility	видимост (ж)	[vídimost]
flight (act of flying)	полет (м)	[pólet]
altitude	височина (ж)	[visoʧiná]
air pocket	въздушна яма (ж)	[vəzdúʃna jáma]
seat	място (с)	[mʲásto]
headphones	слушалки (ж мн)	[sluʃálki]

folding tray (tray table)	прибираща	[pribíraʃta
	се масичка (ж)	se mási tʃka]
airplane window	илюминатор (м)	[ilʲuminátor]
aisle	проход (м)	[próhot]

25. Train

train	влак (м)	[vlak]
commuter train	електрически влак (м)	[elektríʧeski vlak]
express train	бърз влак (м)	[bérz vlak]
diesel locomotive	дизелов локомотив (м)	[dízelof lokomotíf]
steam locomotive	парен локомотив (м)	[páren lokomotíf]
passenger car	вагон (м)	[vagón]
dining car	вагон-ресторант (м)	[vagón-restoránt]
rails	релси (ж мн)	[rélsi]
railroad	железница (ж)	[ʒeléznitsa]
railway tie	траверса (ж)	[travérsa]
platform (railway ~)	платформа (ж)	[platfórma]
track (~ 1, 2, etc.)	коловоз (м)	[kolovós]
semaphore	семафор (м)	[semafór]
station	гара (ж)	[gára]
engineer (train driver)	машинист (м)	[maʃiníst]
porter (of luggage)	носач (м)	[nosáʧ]
car attendant	стюард (м)	[stʲuárt]
passenger	пътник (м)	[pétnik]
conductor	контрольор (м)	[kontrolʲór]
(ticket inspector)		
corridor (in train)	коридор (м)	[koridór]
emergency brake	аварийна спирачка (ж)	[avaríjna spirátʃka]
compartment	купе (с)	[kupé]
berth	легло (с)	[legló]
upper berth	горно легло (с)	[górno legló]
lower berth	долно легло (с)	[dólno legló]
bed linen, bedding	спално бельо (с)	[spálno belʲó]
ticket	билет (м)	[bilét]
schedule	разписание (с)	[raspisánie]
information display	табло (с)	[tabló]
to leave, to depart	заминавам	[zaminávam]
departure (of train)	заминаване (с)	[zaminávane]
to arrive (ab. train)	пристигам	[pristígam]
arrival	пристигане (с)	[pristígane]
to arrive by train	пристигна с влак	[pristígna s vlak]

| to get on the train | качвам се във влак | [kátʃvam se vəf vlak] |
| to get off the train | слизам от влак | [slízam ot vlak] |

train wreck	катастрофа (ж)	[katastrófa]
to derail (vi)	дерайлирам	[derajlíram]
steam locomotive	парен локомотив (м)	[páren lokomotíf]
stoker, fireman	огняр (м)	[ognʲár]
firebox	пещ (м) на локомотив	[peʃt na lokomotíf]
coal	въглища (ж)	[véɡliʃta]

26. Ship

| ship | кораб (м) | [kórap] |
| vessel | плавателен съд (м) | [plavátelen sət] |

steamship	параход (м)	[parahót]
riverboat	моторен кораб (м)	[motóren kórap]
cruise ship	рейсов кораб (м)	[réjsov kórap]
cruiser	крайцер (м)	[krájtser]

yacht	яхта (ж)	[jáhta]
tugboat	влекач (м)	[vlekátʃ]
barge	шлеп (м)	[ʃlep]
ferry	сал (м)	[sal]

| sailing ship | платноходка (ж) | [platnohótka] |
| brigantine | бригантина (ж) | [briɡantína] |

| ice breaker | ледоразбивач (м) | [ledo·razbivátʃ] |
| submarine | подводница (ж) | [podvódnitsa] |

boat (flat-bottomed ~)	лодка (ж)	[lótka]
dinghy	лодка (ж)	[lótka]
lifeboat	спасителна лодка (ж)	[spasítelna lótka]
motorboat	катер (м)	[káter]

captain	капитан (м)	[kapitán]
seaman	матрос (м)	[matrós]
sailor	моряк (м)	[morʲák]
crew	екипаж (м)	[ekipáʒ]

boatswain	боцман (м)	[bótsman]
ship's boy	юнга (м)	[júnɡa]
cook	корабен готвач (м)	[kóraben gotvátʃ]
ship's doctor	корабен лекар (м)	[kóraben lékar]

deck	палуба (ж)	[páluba]
mast	мачта (ж)	[mátʃta]
sail	корабно платно (с)	[kórabno platnó]
hold	трюм (м)	[trʲum]

bow (prow)	**нос** (м)	[nos]
stern	**кърма** (ж)	[kərmá]
oar	**гребло** (с)	[grebló]
screw propeller	**витло** (с)	[vitló]
cabin	**каюта** (ж)	[kajúta]
wardroom	**каюткомпания** (ж)	[kajut kompánija]
engine room	**машинно отделение** (с)	[maʃínno otdelénie]
bridge	**капитански мостик** (м)	[kapitánski móstik]
radio room	**радиобудка** (ж)	[rádiobútka]
wave (radio)	**вълна** (ж)	[vəlná]
logbook	**корабен дневник** (м)	[kóraben dnévnik]
spyglass	**далекоглед** (м)	[dalekoglét]
bell	**камбана** (ж)	[kambána]
flag	**знаме** (с)	[známe]
hawser (mooring ~)	**дебело въже** (с)	[debélo vəʒé]
knot (bowline, etc.)	**възел** (м)	[vézel]
deckrails	**дръжка** (ж)	[dréʃka]
gangway	**трап** (м)	[trap]
anchor	**котва** (ж)	[kótva]
to weigh anchor	**вдигна котва**	[vdígna kótva]
to drop anchor	**хвърля котва**	[hvérlʲa kótva]
anchor chain	**котвена верига** (ж)	[kótvena veríga]
port (harbor)	**пристанище** (с)	[pristániʃte]
quay, wharf	**кей** (м)	[kej]
to berth (moor)	**акостирам**	[akostíram]
to cast off	**отплувам**	[otplúvam]
trip, voyage	**пътешествие** (с)	[pəteʃéstvie]
cruise (sea trip)	**морско пътешествие** (с)	[mórsko pəteʃéstvie]
course (route)	**курс** (м)	[kurs]
route (itinerary)	**маршрут** (м)	[marʃrút]
fairway (safe water channel)	**фарватер** (м)	[farváter]
shallows	**плитчина** (ж)	[plittʃiná]
to run aground	**заседна на плитчина**	[zasédna na plittʃiná]
storm	**буря** (ж)	[búrʲa]
signal	**сигнал** (м)	[signál]
to sink (vi)	**потъвам**	[potévam]
SOS (distress signal)	**SOS**	[sos]
ring buoy	**спасителен пояс** (м)	[spasítilen pójas]

T&P BOOKS

CITY

T&P Books Publishing

27. Urban transportation

bus	автобус (м)	[aftobús]
streetcar	трамвай (м)	[tramváj]
trolley bus	тролей (м)	[troléj]
route (of bus, etc.)	маршрут (м)	[marʃrút]
number (e.g., bus ~)	номер (м)	[nómer]
to go by ...	пътувам с ...	[pətúvam s]
to get on (~ the bus)	качвам се в ...	[kátʃvam se v]
to get off ...	сляза от ...	[slʲáza ot]
stop (e.g., bus ~)	спирка (ж)	[spírka]
next stop	следваща спирка (ж)	[slédvaʃta spírka]
terminus	последна спирка (ж)	[poslédna spírka]
schedule	разписание (с)	[raspisánie]
to wait (vt)	чакам	[tʃákam]
ticket	билет (м)	[bilét]
fare	цена (ж) на билета	[tsená na biléta]
cashier (ticket seller)	касиер (м)	[kasiér]
ticket inspection	контрола (ж)	[kontróla]
ticket inspector	контрольор (м)	[kontrolʲór]
to be late (for ...)	закъснявам	[zakəsnʲávam]
to miss (~ the train, etc.)	закъснея за ...	[zakəsnéja za]
to be in a hurry	бързам	[bérzam]
taxi, cab	такси (с)	[taksí]
taxi driver	таксиметров шофьор (м)	[taksimétrof ʃofʲór]
by taxi	с такси	[s taksí]
taxi stand	пиаца (ж) на такси	[piátsa na taksí]
to call a taxi	извикам такси	[izvíkam taksí]
to take a taxi	взема такси	[vzéma taksí]
traffic	улично движение (с)	[úlitʃno dviʒénie]
traffic jam	задръстване (с)	[zadréstvane]
rush hour	час пик (м)	[tʃas pík]
to park (vi)	паркирам се	[parkíram se]
to park (vt)	паркирам	[párkiram]
parking lot	паркинг (м)	[párking]
subway	метро (с)	[metró]
station	станция (ж)	[stántsija]

to take the subway	пътувам с метро	[pətúvam s metró]
train	влак (м)	[vlak]
train station	гара (ж)	[gára]

28. City. Life in the city

city, town	град (м)	[grat]
capital city	столица (ж)	[stólitsa]
village	село (с)	[sélo]
city map	план (м) на града	[plan na gradá]
downtown	център (м) на града	[tséntər na gradá]
suburb	предградие (с)	[predgrádie]
suburban (adj)	крайградски	[krajgrátski]
outskirts	покрайнина (ж)	[pokrajniná]
environs (suburbs)	околности (мн)	[okólnosti]
city block	квартал (м)	[kvartál]
residential block (area)	жилищен квартал (м)	[ʒíliʃten kvartál]
traffic	движение (с)	[dviʒénie]
traffic lights	светофар (м)	[svetofár]
public transportation	градски транспорт (м)	[grátski transpórt]
intersection	кръстовище (с)	[krəstóviʃte]
crosswalk	зебра (ж)	[zébra]
pedestrian underpass	подлез (м)	[pódlez]
to cross (~ the street)	пресичам	[presítʃam]
pedestrian	пешеходец (м)	[peʃehódets]
sidewalk	тротоар (м)	[trotoàr]
bridge	мост (м)	[most]
embankment (river walk)	кей (м)	[kej]
fountain	фонтан (м)	[fontán]
allée (garden walkway)	алея (ж)	[aléja]
park	парк (м)	[park]
boulevard	булевард (м)	[bulevárt]
square	площад (м)	[ploʃtát]
avenue (wide street)	авеню (с)	[avenʲú]
street	улица (ж)	[úlitsa]
side street	пресечка (ж)	[presétʃka]
dead end	задънена улица (ж)	[zadénena úlitsa]
house	къща (ж)	[kéʃta]
building	сграда (ж)	[zgráda]
skyscraper	небостъргач (м)	[nebostərgátʃ]
facade	фасада (ж)	[fasáda]
roof	покрив (м)	[pókriv]

window	прозорец (м)	[prozórets]
arch	арка (ж)	[árka]
column	колона (ж)	[kolóna]
corner	ъгъл (м)	[ə́gəl]

store window	витрина (ж)	[vitrína]
signboard (store sign, etc.)	табела (ж)	[tabéla]
poster (e.g., playbill)	афиш (м)	[afíʃ]
advertising poster	постер (м)	[póster]
billboard	билборд (м)	[bilbórt]

garbage, trash	боклук (м)	[boklúk]
trash can (public ~)	кошче (с)	[kóʃtʃe]
to litter (vi)	правя боклук	[práv'a boklúk]
garbage dump	сметище (с)	[smétiʃte]

phone booth	телефонна будка (ж)	[telefónna bútka]
lamppost	стълб (м) с фенер	[stəlp s fenér]
bench (park ~)	пейка (ж)	[péjka]

police officer	полицай (м)	[politsáj]
police	полиция (ж)	[polítsija]
beggar	сиромах (м)	[siromáh]
homeless (n)	бездомник (м)	[bezdómnik]

29. Urban institutions

store	магазин (м)	[magazín]
drugstore, pharmacy	аптека (ж)	[aptéka]
eyeglass store	оптика (ж)	[óptika]
shopping mall	търговски център (м)	[tərgófski tséntər]
supermarket	супермаркет (м)	[supermárket]

bakery	хлебарница (ж)	[hlebárnitsa]
baker	фурнаджия (ж)	[furnadʒíja]
pastry shop	сладкарница (ж)	[slatkárnitsa]
grocery store	бакалия (ж)	[bakalíja]
butcher shop	месарница (ж)	[mesárnitsa]

| produce store | магазин (м) за плодове и зеленчуци | [magazín za plodové i zelentʃútsi] |
| market | пазар (м) | [pazár] |

coffee house	кафене (с)	[kafené]
restaurant	ресторант (м)	[restoránt]
pub, bar	бирария (ж)	[biráríja]
pizzeria	пицария (ж)	[pitsaríja]

| hair salon | фризьорски салон (м) | [friz'órski salón] |
| post office | поща (ж) | [póʃta] |

| dry cleaners | химическо чистене (с) | [himítʃesko tʃístene] |
| photo studio | фотостудио (с) | [fotostúdio] |

shoe store	магазин (м) за обувки	[magazín za obúfki]
bookstore	книжарница (ж)	[kniʒárnitsa]
sporting goods store	магазин (м) за спортни стоки	[magazín za spórtni stóki]

clothes repair shop	поправка (ж) на дрехи	[popráfka na dréhi]
formal wear rental	дрехи (ж мн) под наем	[dréhi pot náem]
video rental store	филми (м мн) под наем	[fílmi pot náem]

circus	цирк (м)	[tsirk]
zoo	зоологическа градина (ж)	[zoologítʃeska gradína]
movie theater	кино (с)	[kíno]
museum	музей (м)	[muzéj]
library	библиотека (ж)	[bibliotéka]

theater	театър (м)	[teátər]
opera (opera house)	опера (ж)	[ópera]
nightclub	нощен клуб (м)	[nóʃten klup]
casino	казино (с)	[kazíno]

mosque	джамия (ж)	[dʒamíja]
synagogue	синагога (ж)	[sinagóga]
cathedral	катедрала (ж)	[katedrála]
temple	храм (м)	[hram]
church	църква (ж)	[tsérkva]

college	институт (м)	[institút]
university	университет (м)	[universitét]
school	училище (с)	[utʃíliʃte]

| prefecture | префектура (ж) | [prefektúra] |
| city hall | кметство (с) | [kmétstvo] |

| hotel | хотел (м) | [hotél] |
| bank | банка (ж) | [bánka] |

| embassy | посолство (с) | [posólstvo] |
| travel agency | туристическа агенция (ж) | [turistítʃeska agéntsija] |

| information office | справки (м мн) | [spráfki] |
| currency exchange | обменно бюро (с) | [obménno bʲúro] |

| subway | метро (с) | [metró] |
| hospital | болница (ж) | [bólnitsa] |

| gas station | бензиностанция (ж) | [benzino·stántsija] |
| parking lot | паркинг (м) | [párking] |

30. Signs

signboard (store sign, etc.)	табела (ж)	[tabéla]
notice (door sign, etc.)	надпис (м)	[nádpis]
poster	постер (м)	[póster]
direction sign	указател (м)	[ukazátel]
arrow (sign)	стрелка (ж)	[strelká]
caution	предпазване (с)	[predpázvane]
warning sign	предупреждение (с)	[predupreʒdénie]
to warn (vt)	предупредя	[predupredʲá]
rest day (weekly ~)	почивен ден (м)	[potʃíven dén]
timetable (schedule)	разписание (с)	[raspisánie]
opening hours	работно време (с)	[rabótno vréme]
WELCOME!	ДОБРЕ ДОШЛИ!	[dobré doʃlí]
ENTRANCE	ВХОД	[vhot]
EXIT	ИЗХОД	[íshot]
PUSH	БУТНИ	[butní]
PULL	ДРЪПНИ	[drəpní]
OPEN	ОТВОРЕНО	[otvóreno]
CLOSED	ЗАТВОРЕНО	[zatvóreno]
WOMEN	ЖЕНИ	[ʒení]
MEN	МЪЖЕ	[məʒé]
DISCOUNTS	НАМАЛЕНИЕ	[namalénie]
SALE	РАЗПРОДАЖБА	[rasprodáʒba]
NEW!	НОВА СТОКА	[nóva stóka]
FREE	БЕЗПЛАТНО	[besplátno]
ATTENTION!	ВНИМАНИЕ!	[vnimánie]
NO VACANCIES	НЯМА СВОБОДНИ МЕСТА	[nʲáma svobódni mestá]
RESERVED	РЕЗЕРВИРАНО	[rezervírano]
ADMINISTRATION	АДМИНИСТРАЦИЯ	[administrátsija]
STAFF ONLY	ЗАБРАНЕНО ЗА ВЪНШНИ ЛИЦА	[zabráneno za venʃni lítsa]
BEWARE OF THE DOG!	ЗЛО КУЧЕ	[zlo kútʃe]
NO SMOKING	ПУШЕНЕТО ЗАБРАНЕНО!	[puʃenéto zabráneno]
DO NOT TOUCH!	НЕ ПИПАЙ!	[ne pípaj]
DANGEROUS	ОПАСНО	[opásno]
DANGER	ОПАСНОСТ	[opásnost]
HIGH VOLTAGE	ВИСОКО НАПРЕЖЕНИЕ	[visóko napreʒénie]
NO SWIMMING!	КЪПАНЕТО ЗАБРАНЕНО	[képaneto zabranéno]

OUT OF ORDER	НЕ РАБОТИ	[ne rabóti]
FLAMMABLE	ОГНЕОПАСНО	[ogneopásno]
FORBIDDEN	ЗАБРАНЕНО	[zabranéno]
NO TRESPASSING!	МИНАВАНЕТО ЗАБРАНЕНО	[minávaneto zabranéno]
WET PAINT	ПАЗИ СЕ ОТ БОЯТА	[pazi se ot bojáta]

31. Shopping

to buy (purchase)	купувам	[kupúvam]
purchase	покупка (ж)	[pokúpka]
to go shopping	пазарувам	[pazarúvam]
shopping	пазаруване (с)	[pazarúvane]

| to be open (ab. store) | работя | [rabótʲa] |
| to be closed | затваря се | [zatvárʲa se] |

footwear, shoes	обувки (ж мн)	[obúfki]
clothes, clothing	облекло (с)	[obleklό]
cosmetics	козметика (ж)	[kozmétika]
food products	продукти (м мн)	[prodúkti]
gift, present	подарък (м)	[podárək]

| salesman | продавач (м) | [prodavátʃ] |
| saleswoman | продавачка (ж) | [prodavátʃka] |

check out, cash desk	каса (ж)	[kása]
mirror	огледало (с)	[ogledálo]
counter (store ~)	щанд (м)	[ʃtant]
fitting room	пробна (ж)	[próbna]

to try on	пробвам	[próbvam]
to fit (ab. dress, etc.)	подхождам	[podhóʒdam]
to like (I like …)	харесвам	[harésvam]

price	цена (ж)	[tsená]
price tag	етикет (м)	[etikét]
to cost (vt)	струвам	[strúvam]
How much?	Колко?	[kólko]
discount	намаление (с)	[namalénie]

inexpensive (adj)	нескъп	[neskəp]
cheap (adj)	евтин	[éftin]
expensive (adj)	скъп	[skəp]
It's expensive	Това е скъпо	[tová e skəpo]

rental (n)	под наем (м)	[pot náem]
to rent (~ a tuxedo)	взимам под наем	[vzímam pot náem]
credit (trade credit)	кредит (м)	[krédit]
on credit (adv)	на кредит	[na krédit]

T&P BOOKS

CLOTHING & ACCESSORIES

T&P Books Publishing

32. Outerwear. Coats

clothes	облекло (с)	[oblekló]
outerwear	горни дрехи (ж мн)	[górni dréhi]
winter clothing	зимни дрехи (ж мн)	[zímni dréhi]

coat (overcoat)	палто (с)	[paltó]
fur coat	кожено палто (с)	[kóʒeno paltó]
fur jacket	полушубка (ж)	[poluʃúpka]
down coat	пухено яке (с)	[púheno jáke]

jacket (e.g., leather ~)	яке (с)	[jáke]
raincoat (trenchcoat, etc.)	шлифер (м)	[ʃlífer]
waterproof (adj)	непромокаем	[nepromokáem]

33. Men's & women's clothing

shirt (button shirt)	риза (ж)	[ríza]
pants	панталон (м)	[pantalón]
jeans	дънки, джинси (мн)	[dénki], [dʒínsi]
suit jacket	сако (с)	[sakó]
suit	костюм (м)	[kostʲúm]

dress (frock)	рокля (ж)	[róklʲa]
skirt	пола (ж)	[polá]
blouse	блуза (ж)	[blúza]
knitted jacket (cardigan, etc.)	жилетка (ж)	[ʒilétka]
jacket (of woman's suit)	сако (с)	[sakó]

T-shirt	تениска (ж)	[téniska]
shorts (short trousers)	къси панталони (м мн)	[kési pantalóni]
tracksuit	анцуг (м)	[ántsuk]
bathrobe	хавлиен халат (м)	[havlíen halát]
pajamas	пижама (ж)	[piʒáma]

| sweater | пуловер (м) | [pulóver] |
| pullover | пуловер (м) | [pulóver] |

vest	елек (м)	[elék]
tailcoat	фрак (м)	[frak]
tuxedo	смокинг (м)	[smóking]
uniform	униформа (ж)	[unifórma]
workwear	работно облекло (с)	[rabótno oblekló]

| overalls | гащеризон (м) | [gaʃterizón] |
| coat (e.g., doctor's smock) | бяла престилка (ж) | [bʲála prestílka] |

34. Clothing. Underwear

underwear	бельо (с)	[belʲó]
boxers, briefs	боксер (м)	[boksér]
panties	прашка (ж)	[práʃka]
undershirt (A-shirt)	потник (м)	[pótnik]
socks	чорапи (м мн)	[ʧorápi]

nightdress	нощница (ж)	[nóʃtnitsa]
bra	сутиен (м)	[sutién]
knee highs	чорапи	[ʧorápi
(knee-high socks)	три четвърт (м мн)	tri ʧétvərt]
pantyhose	чорапогащник (м)	[ʧorapogáʃtnik]
stockings (thigh highs)	чорапи (м мн)	[ʧorápi]
bathing suit	бански костюм (м)	[bánski kostʲúm]

35. Headwear

hat	шапка (ж)	[ʃápka]
fedora	шапка (ж)	[ʃápka]
baseball cap	шапка (ж) с козирка	[ʃápka s kozirká]
flatcap	каскет (м)	[kaskét]

beret	барета (ж)	[baréta]
hood	качулка (ж)	[kaʧúlka]
panama hat	панама (ж)	[panáma]
knit cap (knitted hat)	плетена шапка (ж)	[plétena ʃápka]

| headscarf | кърпа (ж) | [kə́rpa] |
| women's hat | шапка (ж) | [ʃápka] |

hard hat	каска (ж)	[káska]
garrison cap	пилотка (ж)	[pilótka]
helmet	шлем (м)	[ʃlem]

| derby | бомбе (с) | [bombé] |
| top hat | цилиндър (м) | [tsilíndər] |

36. Footwear

footwear	обувки (ж мн)	[obúfki]
shoes (men's shoes)	ботинки (мн)	[botínki]
shoes (women's shoes)	обувки (ж мн)	[obúfki]

boots (e.g., cowboy ~)	ботуши (м мн)	[botúʃi]
slippers	чехли (м мн)	[tʃéhli]
tennis shoes (e.g., Nike ~)	маратонки (ж мн)	[maratónki]
sneakers (e.g., Converse ~)	кецове (м мн)	[kétsove]
sandals	сандали (мн)	[sandáli]
cobbler (shoe repairer)	обущар (м)	[obuʃtár]
heel	ток (м)	[tok]
pair (of shoes)	чифт (м)	[tʃift]
shoestring	връзка (ж)	[vréska]
to lace (vt)	връзвам	[vrézvam]
shoehorn	обувалка (ж)	[obuválka]
shoe polish	крем (м) за обувки	[krem za obúfki]

37. Personal accessories

gloves	ръкавици (ж мн)	[rəkavítsi]
mittens	ръкавици (ж мн) с един пърст	[rəkavítsi s edín pərst]
scarf (muffler)	шал (м)	[ʃal]
glasses (eyeglasses)	очила (мн)	[otʃilá]
frame (eyeglass ~)	рамка (ж) за очила	[rámka za otʃilá]
umbrella	чадър (м)	[tʃadér]
walking stick	бастун (м)	[bastún]
hairbrush	четка (ж) за коса	[tʃétka za kosá]
fan	ветрило (с)	[vetrílo]
tie (necktie)	вратовръзка (ж)	[vratovrézka]
bow tie	папийонка (ж)	[papijónka]
suspenders	тиранти (мн)	[tiránti]
handkerchief	носна кърпичка (ж)	[nósna kérpitʃka]
comb	гребен (м)	[grében]
barrette	шнола (ж)	[ʃnóla]
hairpin	фиба (ж)	[fíba]
buckle	катарама (ж)	[kataráma]
belt	колан (м)	[kolán]
shoulder strap	ремък (м)	[rémək]
bag (handbag)	чанта (ж)	[tʃánta]
purse	чантичка (ж)	[tʃántitʃka]
backpack	раница (ж)	[ránitsa]

38. Clothing. Miscellaneous

fashion	мода (ж)	[móda]
in vogue (adj)	модерен	[modéren]
fashion designer	моделиер (м)	[modeliér]

collar	яка (ж)	[jaká]
pocket	джоб (м)	[dʒop]
pocket (as adj)	джобен	[dʒóben]
sleeve	ръкав (м)	[rəkáv]
hanging loop	закачалка (ж)	[zakatʃálka]
fly (on trousers)	копчелък (м)	[koptʃelók]

zipper (fastener)	цип (м)	[tsip]
fastener	закопчалка (ж)	[zakoptʃálka]
button	копче (с)	[kóptʃe]
buttonhole	илик (м)	[ilík]
to come off (ab. button)	откъсна се	[otkésna se]

to sew (vi, vt)	шия	[ʃíja]
to embroider (vi, vt)	бродирам	[brodíram]
embroidery	бродерия (ж)	[brodérija]
sewing needle	игла (ж)	[iglá]
thread	конец (м)	[konéts]
seam	тегел (м)	[tegél]

to get dirty (vi)	изцапам се	[istsápam se]
stain (mark, spot)	петно (с)	[petnó]
to crease, crumple (vi)	смачкам се	[smátʃkam se]
to tear, to rip (vt)	скъсам	[skésam]
clothes moth	молец (м)	[moléts]

39. Personal care. Cosmetics

toothpaste	паста (ж) за зъби	[pásta za zébi]
toothbrush	четка (ж) за зъби	[tʃétka za zébi]
to brush one's teeth	мия си зъбите	[míja si zébite]

razor	бръснач (м)	[brəsnátʃ]
shaving cream	крем (м) за бръснене	[krem za brésnene]
to shave (vi)	бръсна се	[brésna se]

| soap | сапун (м) | [sapún] |
| shampoo | шампоан (м) | [ʃampoán] |

scissors	ножица (ж)	[nóʒitsa]
nail file	пиличка (ж) за нокти	[pílitʃka za nókti]
nail clippers	ножичка (ж) за нокти	[nóʒitʃka za nókti]
tweezers	пинсета (ж)	[pinséta]

cosmetics	козметика (ж)	[kozmétika]
face mask	маска (ж)	[máska]
manicure	маникюр (м)	[manikʲúr]
to have a manicure	правя маникюр	[právʲa manikʲúr]
pedicure	педикюр (м)	[pedikʲúr]
make-up bag	козметична чантичка (ж)	[kozmetítʃna tʃántitʃka]
face powder	пудра (ж)	[púdra]
powder compact	пудриера (ж)	[pudriéra]
blusher	руж (ж)	[ruʃ]
perfume (bottled)	парфюм (м)	[parfʲúm]
toilet water (lotion)	тоалетна вода (ж)	[toalétna vodá]
lotion	лосион (м)	[losión]
cologne	одеколон (м)	[odekolón]
eyeshadow	сенки (ж мн) за очи	[sénki za otʃí]
eyeliner	молив (м) за очи	[móliv za otʃí]
mascara	спирала (ж)	[spirála]
lipstick	червило (с)	[tʃervílo]
nail polish, enamel	лак (м) за нокти	[lak za nókti]
hair spray	лак (м) за коса	[lak za kosá]
deodorant	дезодорант (м)	[dezodoránt]
cream	крем (м)	[krem]
face cream	крем (м) за лице	[krem za litsé]
hand cream	крем (м) за ръце	[krem za rətsé]
anti-wrinkle cream	крем (м) срещу бръчки	[krem sreʃtú brétʃki]
day cream	дневен крем (м)	[dnéven krem]
night cream	нощен крем (м)	[nóʃten krem]
day (as adj)	дневен	[dnéven]
night (as adj)	нощен	[nóʃten]
tampon	тампон (м)	[tampón]
toilet paper (toilet roll)	тоалетна хартия (ж)	[toalétna hartíja]
hair dryer	сешоар (м)	[seʃoár]

40. Watches. Clocks

watch (wristwatch)	часовник (м)	[tʃasóvnik]
dial	циферблат (м)	[tsiferblát]
hand (of clock, watch)	стрелка (ж)	[strelká]
metal watch band	гривна (ж)	[grívna]
watch strap	каишка (ж)	[kaíʃka]
battery	батерия (ж)	[batérija]
to be dead (battery)	батерията се изтощи	[batérijata se istoʃtí]
to change a battery	сменям батерия	[sménʲam batérija]
to run fast	избързвам	[izbérzvam]

to run slow	изоставам	[izostávam]
wall clock	стенен часовник (м)	[sténen ʧasóvnik]
hourglass	пясъчен часовник (м)	[pʲásəʧen ʧasóvnik]
sundial	слънчев часовник (м)	[slénʧev ʧasóvnik]
alarm clock	будилник (м)	[budílnik]
watchmaker	часовникар (м)	[ʧasovnikár]
to repair (vt)	поправям	[poprávʲam]

T&P BOOKS

EVERYDAY EXPERIENCE

T&P Books Publishing

41. Money

money	пари (мн)	[parí]
currency exchange	обмяна (ж)	[obmʲána]
exchange rate	курс (м)	[kurs]
ATM	банкомат (м)	[bankomát]
coin	монета (ж)	[monéta]

| dollar | долар (м) | [dólar] |
| euro | евро (с) | [évro] |

lira	лира (ж)	[líra]
Deutschmark	марка (ж)	[márka]
franc	франк (м)	[frank]
pound sterling	британска лира (ж)	[británska líra]
yen	йена (ж)	[jéna]

debt	дълг (м)	[dəlk]
debtor	длъжник (м)	[dləʒník]
to lend (money)	давам на заем	[dávam na záem]
to borrow (vi, vt)	взема на заем	[vzéma na záem]

bank	банка (ж)	[bánka]
account	сметка (ж)	[smétka]
to deposit (vt)	депозирам	[depozíram]
to deposit into the account	внеса в сметка	[vnesá v smétka]
to withdraw (vt)	тегля от сметката	[téglʲa ot smétkata]

credit card	кредитна карта (ж)	[kréditna kárta]
cash	налични пари (мн)	[nalíʧni parí]
check	чек (м)	[ʧek]
to write a check	подпиша чек	[potpíʃa ʧek]
checkbook	чекова книжка (ж)	[ʧékova kníʃka]

wallet	портфейл (м)	[portféjl]
change purse	портмоне (с)	[portmoné]
safe	сейф (м)	[sejf]

heir	наследник (м)	[naslédnik]
inheritance	наследство (с)	[naslétstvo]
fortune (wealth)	състояние (с)	[səstojánie]

lease	наем (м)	[náem]
rent (money)	наем (м)	[náem]
to rent (sth from sb)	наемам	[naémam]
price	цена (ж)	[tsená]

cost	стойност (ж)	[stójnost]
sum	сума (ж)	[súma]
to spend (vt)	харча	[hártʃa]
expenses	разходи (м мн)	[ráshodi]
to economize (vi, vt)	пестя	[pestʲá]
economical	пестелив	[pestelíf]
to pay (vi, vt)	плащам	[pláʃtam]
payment	плащане (с)	[pláʃtane]
change (give the ~)	ресто (с)	[résto]
tax	данък (м)	[dánək]
fine	глоба (ж)	[glóba]
to fine (vt)	глобявам	[globʲávam]

42. Post. Postal service

post office	поща (ж)	[póʃta]
mail (letters, etc.)	поща (ж)	[póʃta]
mailman	пощальон (м)	[poʃtalʲón]
opening hours	работно време (с)	[rabótno vréme]
letter	писмо (с)	[pismó]
registered letter	препоръчано писмо (с)	[preporétʃano pismó]
postcard	картичка (ж)	[kártitʃka]
telegram	телеграма (ж)	[telegráma]
package (parcel)	колет (м)	[kolét]
money transfer	паричен превод (м)	[parítʃen prévot]
to receive (vt)	получа	[polútʃa]
to send (vt)	изпратя	[isprátʲa]
sending	изпращане (с)	[ispráʃtane]
address	адрес (м)	[adrés]
ZIP code	пощенски код (м)	[póʃtenski kot]
sender	подател (м)	[podátel]
receiver	получател (м)	[polutʃátel]
name (first name)	име (с)	[íme]
surname (last name)	фамилия (ж)	[famílija]
postage rate	тарифа (ж)	[tarífa]
standard (adj)	обикновен	[obiknovén]
economical (adj)	икономичен	[ikonomítʃen]
weight	тегло (с)	[tegló]
to weigh (~ letters)	претеглям	[pretéglʲam]
envelope	плик (м)	[plik]
postage stamp	марка (ж)	[márka]

43. Banking

bank	банка (ж)	[bánka]
branch (of bank, etc.)	клон (м)	[klon]
bank clerk, consultant	консултант (м)	[konsultánt]
manager (director)	управител (м)	[uprável]
bank account	сметка (ж)	[smétka]
account number	номер (м) на сметка	[nómer na smétka]
checking account	текуща сметка (ж)	[tekúʃta smétka]
savings account	спестовна сметка (ж)	[spestóvna smétka]
to open an account	откривам сметка	[otkrívam smétka]
to close the account	закривам сметка	[zakrívam smétka]
to deposit into the account	депозирам в сметка	[depozíram f smétka]
to withdraw (vt)	тегля от сметката	[téglʲa ot smétkata]
deposit	влог (м)	[vlok]
to make a deposit	направя влог	[naprávʲa vlok]
wire transfer	превод (м)	[prévot]
to wire, to transfer	направя превод	[naprávʲa prévot]
sum	сума (ж)	[súma]
How much?	Колко?	[kólko]
signature	подпис (м)	[pótpis]
to sign (vt)	подпиша	[potpíʃa]
credit card	кредитна карта (ж)	[kréditna kárta]
code (PIN code)	код (м)	[kot]
credit card number	номер (м)	[nómer
	на кредитна карта	na kréditna kárta]
ATM	банкомат (м)	[bankomát]
check	чек (м)	[tʃek]
to write a check	подпиша чек	[potpíʃa tʃek]
checkbook	чекова книжка (ж)	[tʃékova kníʃka]
loan (bank ~)	кредит (м)	[krédit]
to apply for a loan	кандидатствам	[kandidátstvam
	за кредит	za krédit]
to get a loan	взимам кредит	[vzímam krédit]
to give a loan	предоставям кредит	[predostávʲam krédit]
guarantee	гаранция (ж)	[garántsija]

44. Telephone. Phone conversation

telephone	телефон (м)	[telefón]
cell phone	мобилен телефон (м)	[mobílen telefón]

answering machine	телефонен секретар (м)	[telefónen sekretár]
to call (by phone)	обаждам се	[obáʒdam se]
phone call	обаждане (с)	[obáʒdane]

to dial a number	набирам номер	[nabíram nómer]
Hello!	Ало!	[álo]
to ask (vt)	питам	[pítam]
to answer (vi, vt)	отговарям	[otgovárʲam]

to hear (vt)	чувам	[tʃúvam]
well (adv)	добре	[dobré]
not well (adv)	лошо	[lóʃo]
noises (interference)	шумове (м мн)	[ʃúmove]

receiver	слушалка (ж)	[sluʃálka]
to pick up (~ the phone)	вдигам слушалката	[vdígam sluʃálkata]
to hang up (~ the phone)	затварям телефона	[zatvárʲam telefóna]
busy (engaged)	заета	[zaéta]
to ring (ab. phone)	звъня	[zvənʲá]
telephone book	телефонен справочник (м)	[telefónen spravótʃnik]

local (adj)	селищен	[séliʃten]
local call	селищен разговор (м)	[séliʃten rázgovor]
long distance (~ call)	междуградски	[meʒdugrátski]
long-distance call	междуградски разговор (м)	[meʒdugrátski rázgovor]

international (adj)	международен	[meʒdunaróden]
international call	международен разговор (м)	[meʒdunaróden rázgovor]

45. Cell phone

cell phone	мобилен телефон (м)	[mobílen telefón]
display	дисплей (м)	[displéj]
button	бутон (м)	[butón]
SIM card	SIM-карта (ж)	[sim-kárta]

battery	батерия (ж)	[batérija]
to be dead (battery)	изтощавам	[iztoʃtávam]
charger	зареждащо устройство (с)	[zaréʒdaʃto ustrójstvo]

menu	меню (с)	[menʲú]
settings	настройки (ж мн)	[nastrójki]
tune (melody)	мелодия (ж)	[melódija]
to select (vt)	избера	[izberá]

calculator	калкулатор (м)	[kalkulátor]
voice mail	телефонен секретар (м)	[telefónen sekretár]

alarm clock	будилник (м)	[budílnik]
contacts	телефонен справочник (м)	[telefónen spravótʃnik]
SMS (text message)	SMS съобщение (с)	[esemés səobʃténie]
subscriber	абонат (м)	[abonát]

46. Stationery

ballpoint pen	химикалка (ж)	[himikálka]
fountain pen	перодръжка (ж)	[perodrə́ʒka]
pencil	молив (м)	[móliv]
highlighter	маркер (м)	[márker]
felt-tip pen	флумастер (м)	[flumáster]
notepad	тефтер (м)	[teftér]
agenda (diary)	ежедневник (м)	[eʒednévnik]
ruler	линийка (ж)	[línijka]
calculator	калкулатор (м)	[kalkulátor]
eraser	гума (ж)	[gúma]
thumbtack	кабърче (с)	[kábərtʃe]
paper clip	кламер (м)	[klámer]
glue	лепило (с)	[lepílo]
stapler	телбод (м)	[telbót]
hole punch	перфоратор (м)	[perforátor]
pencil sharpener	острилка (ж)	[ostrílka]

47. Foreign languages

language	език (м)	[ezík]
foreign (adj)	чужд	[tʃuʒd]
foreign language	чужд език (м)	[tʃuʒd ezík]
to study (vt)	изучавам	[izutʃávam]
to learn (language, etc.)	уча	[útʃa]
to read (vi, vt)	чета	[tʃeta]
to speak (vi, vt)	говоря	[govórʲa]
to understand (vt)	разбирам	[razbíram]
to write (vt)	пиша	[píʃa]
fast (adv)	бързо	[bérzo]
slowly (adv)	бавно	[bávno]
fluently (adv)	свободно	[svobódno]
rules	правила (с мн)	[pravilá]
grammar	граматика (ж)	[gramátika]

vocabulary	лексика (ж)	[léksika]
phonetics	фонетика (ж)	[fonétika]
textbook	учебник (м)	[utʃébnik]
dictionary	речник (м)	[rétʃnik]
teach-yourself book	самоучител (м)	[samoutʃítel]
phrasebook	разговорник (м)	[razgovórnik]
cassette, tape	касета (ж)	[kaséta]
videotape	видеокасета (ж)	[video·kaséta]
CD, compact disc	CD диск (м)	[sidí disk]
DVD	DVD (м)	[dividí]
alphabet	алфавит (м)	[alfavít]
to spell (vt)	спелувам	[spelúvam]
pronunciation	произношение (с)	[proiznoʃénie]
accent	акцент (м)	[aktsént]
with an accent	с акцент	[s aktsént]
without an accent	без акцент	[bez aktsént]
word	дума (ж)	[dúma]
meaning	смисъл (м)	[smísəl]
course (e.g., a French ~)	курсове (м мн)	[kúrsove]
to sign up	запиша се	[zapíʃa se]
teacher	преподавател (м)	[prepodavátel]
translation (process)	превод (м)	[prévot]
translation (text, etc.)	превод (м)	[prévot]
translator	преводач (м)	[prevodátʃ]
interpreter	преводач (м)	[prevodátʃ]
polyglot	полиглот (м)	[poliglót]
memory	памет (ж)	[pámet]

BOOKS

MEALS. RESTAURANT

T&P Books Publishing

48. Table setting

spoon	лъжица (ж)	[ləʒítsa]
knife	нож (м)	[noʒ]
fork	вилица (ж)	[vílitsa]

cup (e.g., coffee ~)	чаша (ж)	[ʧáʃa]
plate (dinner ~)	чиния (ж)	[ʧiníja]
saucer	чинийка (ж)	[ʧiníjka]
napkin (on table)	салфетка (ж)	[salfétka]
toothpick	клечка (ж) за зъби	[kléʧka za zébi]

49. Restaurant

restaurant	ресторант (м)	[restoránt]
coffee house	кафене (с)	[kafené]
pub, bar	бар (м)	[bar]
tearoom	чаен салон (м)	[ʧáen salón]

waiter	сервитьор (м)	[serviti̯ór]
waitress	сервитьорка (ж)	[serviti̯órka]
bartender	барман (м)	[bárman]
menu	меню (с)	[meni̯ú]
wine list	карта (ж) на виното	[kárta na vínoto]
to book a table	резервирам масичка	[rezervíram másiʧka]
course, dish	ядене (с)	[jádene]
to order (meal)	поръчам	[poréʧam]
to make an order	правя поръчка	[právi̯a poréʧka]

aperitif	аперитив (м)	[aperitív]
appetizer	мезе (с)	[mezé]
dessert	десерт (м)	[desért]

check	сметка (ж)	[smétka]
to pay the check	плащам сметка	[pláʃtam smétka]
to give change	връщам ресто	[vréʃtam résto]
tip	бакшиш (м)	[bakʃíʃ]

50. Meals

| food | храна (ж) | [hraná] |
| to eat (vi, vt) | ям | [jam] |

breakfast	закуска (ж)	[zakúska]
to have breakfast	закусвам	[zakúsvam]
lunch	обяд (м)	[obʲát]
to have lunch	обядвам	[obʲádvam]
dinner	вечеря (ж)	[vetʃérʲa]
to have dinner	вечерям	[vetʃérʲam]

| appetite | апетит (м) | [apetít] |
| Enjoy your meal! | Добър апетит! | [dobér apetít] |

to open (~ a bottle)	отварям	[otvárʲam]
to spill (liquid)	излея	[izléja]
to spill out (vi)	излея се	[izléja se]

to boil (vi)	вря	[vrʲa]
to boil (vt)	варя до кипване	[varʲá do kípvane]
boiled (~ water)	преварен	[prevarén]
to chill, cool down (vt)	охладя	[ohladʲá]
to chill (vi)	изстудявам се	[isstudʲávam se]

| taste, flavor | вкус (м) | [fkus] |
| aftertaste | привкус (м) | [prífkus] |

to slim down (lose weight)	отслабвам	[otslábvam]
diet	диета (ж)	[diéta]
vitamin	витамин (м)	[vitamín]
calorie	калория (ж)	[kalórija]
vegetarian (n)	вегетарианец (м)	[vegetariánets]
vegetarian (adj)	вегетариански	[vegetariánski]

fats (nutrient)	мазнини (ж мн)	[maznіní]
proteins	белтъчини (ж мн)	[beltətʃіní]
carbohydrates	въглехидрати (м мн)	[vəglehidráti]
slice (of lemon, ham)	резенче (с)	[rézentʃe]
piece (of cake, pie)	парче (с)	[partʃé]
crumb	троха (ж)	[trohá]
(of bread, cake, etc.)		

51. Cooked dishes

course, dish	ястие (с)	[jástie]
cuisine	кухня (ж)	[kúhnʲa]
recipe	рецепта (ж)	[retsépta]
portion	порция (ж)	[pórtsija]

| salad | салата (ж) | [saláta] |
| soup | супа (ж) | [súpa] |

| clear soup (broth) | бульон (м) | [buljón] |
| sandwich (bread) | сандвич (м) | [sándvitʃ] |

fried eggs	пържени яйца (с мн)	[pérʒeni jajtsá]
hamburger (beefburger)	хамбургер (м)	[hámburger]
beefsteak	бифтек (м)	[biftěk]

side dish	гарнитура (ж)	[garnitúra]
spaghetti	спагети (мн)	[spagéti]
mashed potatoes	картофено пюре (с)	[kartófeno pʲuré]
pizza	пица (ж)	[pítsa]
porridge (oatmeal, etc.)	каша (ж)	[káʃa]
omelet	омлет (м)	[omlét]

boiled (e.g., ~ beef)	варен	[varén]
smoked (adj)	пушен	[púʃen]
fried (adj)	пържен	[pérʒen]
dried (adj)	сушен	[suʃén]
frozen (adj)	замразен	[zamrazén]
pickled (adj)	маринован	[marinóvan]

sweet (sugary)	сладък	[sládək]
salty (adj)	солен	[solén]
cold (adj)	студен	[studén]
hot (adj)	горещ	[goréʃt]
bitter (adj)	горчив	[gortʃív]
tasty (adj)	вкусен	[fkúsen]

to cook in boiling water	готвя	[gótvʲa]
to cook (dinner)	готвя	[gótvʲa]
to fry (vt)	пържа	[pérʒa]
to heat up (food)	затоплям	[zatóplʲam]

to salt (vt)	соля	[solʲá]
to pepper (vt)	слагам пипер	[slágam pipér]
to grate (vt)	стъргам	[stérgam]
peel (n)	кожа (ж)	[kóʒa]
to peel (vt)	беля	[bélʲa]

52. Food

meat	месо (с)	[mesó]
chicken	кокошка (ж)	[kokóʃka]
Rock Cornish hen (poussin)	пиле (с)	[píle]
duck	патица (ж)	[pátitsa]
goose	гъска (ж)	[géska]
game	дивеч (ж)	[dívetʃ]
turkey	пуйка (ж)	[pújka]

pork	свинско (с)	[svínsko]
veal	телешко месо (с)	[téleʃko mesó]
lamb	агнешко (с)	[ágneʃko]

| beef | говеждо (c) | [govéʒdo] |
| rabbit | питомен заек (м) | [pítomen záek] |

| sausage (bologna, etc.) | салам (м) | [salám] |
| vienna sausage (frankfurter) | кренвирш (м) | [krénvirʃ] |

bacon	бекон (м)	[bekón]
ham	шунка (ж)	[ʃúnka]
gammon	бут (м)	[but]

pâté	пастет (м)	[pastét]
liver	черен дроб (м)	[tʃéren drop]
hamburger (ground beef)	кайма (ж)	[kajmá]
tongue	език (м)	[ezík]

egg	яйце (c)	[jajtsé]
eggs	яйца (c мн)	[jajtsá]
egg white	белтък (м)	[belték]
egg yolk	жълтък (м)	[ʒəlték]

fish	риба (ж)	[ríba]
seafood	морски продукти (м мн)	[mórski prodúkti]
caviar	хайвер (м)	[hajvér]

crab	морски рак (м)	[mórski rak]
shrimp	скарида (ж)	[skarída]
oyster	стрида (ж)	[strída]
spiny lobster	лангуста (ж)	[langústa]
octopus	октопод (м)	[oktopót]
squid	калмар (м)	[kalmár]

sturgeon	есетра (ж)	[esétra]
salmon	сьомга (ж)	[sʲómga]
halibut	палтус (м)	[páltus]

cod	треска (ж)	[tréska]
mackerel	скумрия (ж)	[skumríja]
tuna	риба тон (м)	[ríba ton]
eel	змиорка (ж)	[zmiórka]

trout	пъстърва (ж)	[pəstérva]
sardine	сардина (ж)	[sardína]
pike	щука (ж)	[ʃtúka]
herring	селда (ж)	[sélda]

bread	хляб (м)	[hlʲap]
cheese	кашкавал (м)	[kaʃkavál]
sugar	захар (ж)	[záhar]
salt	сол (ж)	[sol]

| rice | ориз (м) | [oríz] |
| pasta (macaroni) | макарони (мн) | [makaróni] |

noodles	юфка (ж)	[jufká]
butter	краве масло (с)	[kráve masló]
vegetable oil	олио (с)	[ólio]
sunflower oil	слънчогледово масло (с)	[sləntʃoglédovo máslo]
margarine	маргарин (м)	[margarín]
olives	маслини (ж мн)	[maslíni]
olive oil	зехтин (м)	[zehtín]
milk	мляко (с)	[mlʲáko]
condensed milk	сгъстено мляко (с)	[sgəsténo mlʲáko]
yogurt	йогурт (м)	[jógurt]
sour cream	сметана (ж)	[smetána]
cream (of milk)	каймак (м)	[kajmák]
mayonnaise	майонеза (ж)	[majonéza]
buttercream	крем (м)	[krem]
groats (barley ~, etc.)	грис, булгур (м)	[gris], [bulgúr]
flour	брашно (с)	[braʃnó]
canned food	консерви (ж мн)	[konsérvi]
cornflakes	царевичен флейкс (м)	[tsárevitʃen flejks]
honey	мед (м)	[met]
jam	конфитюр (м)	[konfitʲúr]
chewing gum	дъвка (ж)	[défka]

53. Drinks

water	вода (ж)	[vodá]
drinking water	питейна вода (ж)	[pitéjna vodá]
mineral water	минерална вода (ж)	[minerálna vodá]
still (adj)	негазирана	[negazíran]
carbonated (adj)	газирана	[gazíran]
sparkling (adj)	газирана	[gazíran]
ice	лед (м)	[let]
with ice	с лед	[s let]
non-alcoholic (adj)	безалкохолен	[bezalkohólen]
soft drink	безалкохолна напитка (ж)	[bezalkohólna napítka]
refreshing drink	разхладителна напитка (ж)	[rashladítelna napítka]
lemonade	лимонада (ж)	[limonáda]
liquors	спиртни напитки (ж мн)	[spírtni napítki]
wine	вино (с)	[víno]
white wine	бяло вино (с)	[bʲálo víno]

red wine	червено вино (c)	[ʧervéno víno]
liqueur	ликьор (м)	[likʲór]
champagne	шампанско (c)	[ʃampánsko]
vermouth	вермут (м)	[vermút]

whiskey	уиски (c)	[wíski]
vodka	водка (ж)	[vótka]
gin	джин (м)	[dʒin]
cognac	коняк (м)	[konʲák]
rum	ром (м)	[rom]

coffee	кафе (c)	[kafé]
black coffee	черно кафе (c)	[ʧérno kafé]
coffee with milk	кафе (c) с мляко	[kafé s mlʲáko]
cappuccino	кафе (c) със сметана	[kafé səs smetána]
instant coffee	разтворимо кафе (c)	[rastvorímo kafé]

milk	мляко (c)	[mlʲáko]
cocktail	коктейл (м)	[koktéjl]
milkshake	млечен коктейл (м)	[mléʧen koktéjl]

juice	сок (м)	[sok]
tomato juice	доматен сок (м)	[domáten sok]
orange juice	портокалов сок (м)	[portokálov sok]
freshly squeezed juice	фреш (м)	[freʃ]

beer	бира (ж)	[bíra]
light beer	светла бира (ж)	[svétla bíra]
dark beer	тъмна бира (ж)	[témna bíra]

tea	чай (м)	[ʧaj]
black tea	черен чай (м)	[ʧéren ʧaj]
green tea	зелен чай (м)	[zelén ʧaj]

54. Vegetables

vegetables	зеленчуци (м мн)	[zelenʧútsi]
greens	зарзават (м)	[zarzavát]

tomato	домат (м)	[domát]
cucumber	краставица (ж)	[krástavitsa]
carrot	морков (м)	[mórkof]
potato	картофи (мн)	[kartófi]
onion	лук (м)	[luk]
garlic	чесън (м)	[ʧésən]

cabbage	зеле (c)	[zéle]
cauliflower	карфиол (м)	[karfiól]
Brussels sprouts	брюкселско зеле (c)	[brʲúkselsko zéle]
broccoli	броколи (c)	[brókoli]

beet	цвекло (с)	[tsveklό]
eggplant	патладжан (м)	[patladʒán]
zucchini	тиквичка (ж)	[tíkvitʃka]
pumpkin	тиква (ж)	[tíkva]
turnip	ряпа (ж)	[rʲápa]

parsley	магданоз (м)	[magdanόz]
dill	копър (м)	[kόpər]
lettuce	салата (ж)	[saláta]
celery	целина (ж)	[tsélina]
asparagus	аспержа (ж)	[aspérʒa]
spinach	спанак (м)	[spanák]

pea	грах (м)	[grah]
beans	боб (м)	[bop]
corn (maize)	царевица (ж)	[tsárevitsa]
kidney bean	фасул (м)	[fasúl]

bell pepper	пипер (м)	[pipér]
radish	репичка (ж)	[répitʃka]
artichoke	ангинар (м)	[anginár]

55. Fruits. Nuts

fruit	плод (м)	[plot]
apple	ябълка (ж)	[jábəlka]
pear	круша (ж)	[krúʃa]
lemon	лимон (м)	[limόn]
orange	портокал (м)	[portokál]
strawberry (garden ~)	ягода (ж)	[jágoda]

mandarin	мандарина (ж)	[mandarína]
plum	слива (ж)	[slíva]
peach	праскова (ж)	[práskova]
apricot	кайсия (ж)	[kajsíja]
raspberry	малина (ж)	[malína]
pineapple	ананас (м)	[ananás]

banana	банан (м)	[banán]
watermelon	диня (ж)	[dínʲa]
grape	грозде (с)	[grόzde]
sour cherry	вишна (ж)	[víʃna]
sweet cherry	череша (ж)	[tʃeréʃa]
melon	пъпеш (м)	[pə́peʃ]

grapefruit	грейпфрут (м)	[gréjpfrut]
avocado	авокадо (с)	[avokádo]
papaya	папая (ж)	[papája]
mango	манго (с)	[mángo]
pomegranate	нар (м)	[nar]

redcurrant	червено френско грозде (c)	[tʃervéno frénsko grózde]
blackcurrant	черно френско грозде (c)	[tʃérno frénsko grózde]
gooseberry	цариградско грозде (c)	[tsarigrátsko grózde]
bilberry	боровинки (ж мн)	[borovínki]
blackberry	къпина (ж)	[kəpína]
raisin	стафиди (ж мн)	[stafídi]
fig	смокиня (ж)	[smokínʲa]
date	фурма (ж)	[furmá]
peanut	фъстък (м)	[fəsték]
almond	бадем (м)	[badém]
walnut	орех (м)	[óreh]
hazelnut	лешник (м)	[léʃnik]
coconut	кокосов орех (м)	[kokósov óreh]
pistachios	шамфъстъци (м мн)	[ʃamfəstétsi]

56. Bread. Candy

bakers' confectionery (pastry)	сладкарски изделия (с мн)	[slatkárski izdélija]
bread	хляб (м)	[hlʲap]
cookies	бисквити (ж мн)	[biskvíti]
chocolate (n)	шоколад (м)	[ʃokolát]
chocolate (as adj)	шоколадов	[ʃokoládov]
candy (wrapped)	бонбон (м)	[bonbón]
cake (e.g., cupcake)	паста (ж)	[pásta]
cake (e.g., birthday ~)	торта (ж)	[tórta]
pie (e.g., apple ~)	пирог (м)	[pirók]
filling (for cake, pie)	плънка (ж)	[plénka]
jam (whole fruit jam)	сладко (c)	[slátko]
marmalade	мармалад (м)	[marmalát]
wafers	вафли (ж мн)	[váfli]
ice-cream	сладолед (м)	[sladolét]

57. Spices

salt	сол (ж)	[sol]
salty (adj)	солен	[solén]
to salt (vt)	соля	[solʲá]
black pepper	черен пипер (м)	[tʃéren pipér]
red pepper (milled ~)	червен пипер (м)	[tʃervén pipér]

mustard	**горчица** (ж)	[gortʃítsa]
horseradish	**хрян** (м)	[hrʲan]
condiment	**подправка** (ж)	[podpráfka]
spice	**подправка** (ж)	[podpráfka]
sauce	**сос** (м)	[sos]
vinegar	**оцет** (м)	[otsét]
anise	**анасон** (м)	[anasón]
basil	**босилек** (м)	[bosílek]
cloves	**карамфил** (м)	[karamfíl]
ginger	**джинджифил** (м)	[dʒindʒifíl]
coriander	**кориандър** (м)	[koriándər]
cinnamon	**канела** (ж)	[kanéla]
sesame	**сусам** (м)	[susám]
bay leaf	**дафинов лист** (м)	[dafínov list]
paprika	**червен пипер** (м)	[tʃervén pipér]
caraway	**черен тмин** (м)	[tʃéren tmin]
saffron	**шафран** (м)	[ʃafrán]

BOOKS

T&P

PERSONAL
INFORMATION. FAMILY

T&P Books Publishing

58. Personal information. Forms

name (first name)	**име** (с)	[íme]
surname (last name)	**фамилия** (ж)	[famílija]
date of birth	**дата** (ж) **на раждане**	[dáta na ráʒdane]
place of birth	**място** (с) **на раждане**	[mʲásto na ráʒdane]
nationality	**националност** (ж)	[natsionálnost]
place of residence	**местожителство** (с)	[mestoʒítelstvo]
country	**страна** (ж)	[straná]
profession (occupation)	**професия** (ж)	[profésija]
gender, sex	**пол** (м)	[pol]
height	**ръст** (м)	[rəst]
weight	**тегло** (с)	[tegló]

59. Family members. Relatives

mother	**майка** (ж)	[májka]
father	**баща** (м)	[baʃtá]
son	**син** (м)	[sin]
daughter	**дъщеря** (ж)	[dəʃterʲá]
younger daughter	**по-малка дъщеря** (ж)	[po-málka dəʃterʲá]
younger son	**по-малък син** (м)	[po-málək sin]
eldest daughter	**по-голяма дъщеря** (ж)	[po-golʲáma dəʃterʲá]
eldest son	**по-голям син** (м)	[po-golʲám sin]
brother	**брат** (м)	[brat]
sister	**сестра** (ж)	[sestrá]
cousin (masc.)	**братовчед** (м)	[bratovtʃét]
cousin (fem.)	**братовчедка** (ж)	[bratovtʃétka]
mom, mommy	**мама** (ж)	[máma]
dad, daddy	**татко** (м)	[tátko]
parents	**родители** (м мн)	[rodíteli]
child	**дете** (с)	[deté]
children	**деца** (с мн)	[detsá]
grandmother	**баба** (ж)	[bába]
grandfather	**дядо** (м)	[dʲádo]
grandson	**внук** (м)	[vnuk]
granddaughter	**внучка** (ж)	[vnútʃka]
grandchildren	**внуци** (м мн)	[vnútsi]

uncle	вуйчо (м)	[vújtʃo]
aunt	леля (ж)	[lélʲa]
nephew	племенник (м)	[plémennik]
niece	племенница (ж)	[plémennitsa]
mother-in-law (wife's mother)	тъща (ж)	[téʃta]
father-in-law (husband's father)	свекър (м)	[svékər]
son-in-law (daughter's husband)	зет (м)	[zet]
stepmother	мащеха (ж)	[máʃteha]
stepfather	пастрок (м)	[pástrok]
infant	кърмаче (с)	[kərmátʃe]
baby (infant)	бебе (с)	[bébe]
little boy, kid	момченце (с)	[momtʃéntse]
wife	жена (ж)	[ʒená]
husband	мъж (м)	[məʒ]
spouse (husband)	съпруг (м)	[səprúk]
spouse (wife)	съпруга (ж)	[səprúga]
married (masc.)	женен	[ʒénen]
married (fem.)	омъжена	[oméʒena]
single (unmarried)	неженен	[neʒénen]
bachelor	ерген (м)	[ergén]
divorced (masc.)	разведен	[razvéden]
widow	вдовица (ж)	[vdovítsa]
widower	вдовец (м)	[vdovéts]
relative	роднина (м, ж)	[rodnina]
close relative	близък роднина (м)	[blízək rodnína]
distant relative	далечен роднина (м)	[dalétʃen rodnína]
relatives	роднини (мн)	[rodníni]
orphan (boy or girl)	сирак (м)	[sirák]
guardian (of a minor)	опекун (м)	[opekún]
to adopt (a boy)	осиновявам	[osinovʲávam]
to adopt (a girl)	осиновявам момиче	[osinovʲávam momítʃe]

60. Friends. Coworkers

friend (masc.)	приятел (м)	[prijátel]
friend (fem.)	приятелка (ж)	[prijátelka]
friendship	приятелство (с)	[prijátelstvo]
to be friends	дружа	[druʒá]
buddy (masc.)	приятел (м)	[prijátel]
buddy (fem.)	приятелка (ж)	[prijátelka]

partner	партньор (м)	[partnʲór]
chief (boss)	шеф (м)	[ʃef]
superior (n)	началник (м)	[natʃálnik]
subordinate (n)	подчинен (м)	[podtʃinén]
colleague	колега (м, ж)	[koléga]

acquaintance (person)	познат (м)	[poznát]
fellow traveler	спътник (м)	[spétnik]
classmate	съученик (м)	[səutʃeník]

neighbor (masc.)	съсед (м)	[səsét]
neighbor (fem.)	съседка (ж)	[səsétka]
neighbors	съседи (м мн)	[səsédi]

BOOKS

T&P

HUMAN BODY.
MEDICINE

T&P Books Publishing

head	глава (ж)	[glavá]
face	лице (с)	[litsé]
nose	нос (м)	[nos]
mouth	уста (ж)	[ustá]

eye	око (с)	[okó]
eyes	очи (с мн)	[otʃí]
pupil	зеница (ж)	[zénitsa]
eyebrow	вежда (ж)	[véʒda]
eyelash	мигла (ж)	[mígla]
eyelid	клепач (м)	[klepátʃ]

tongue	език (м)	[ezík]
tooth	зъб (м)	[zəp]
lips	устни (ж мн)	[ústni]
cheekbones	скули (ж мн)	[skúli]
gum	венец (м)	[venéts]
palate	небце (с)	[nebtsé]

nostrils	ноздри (ж мн)	[nózdri]
chin	брадичка (ж)	[bradítʃka]
jaw	челюст (ж)	[tʃélʲust]
cheek	буза (ж)	[búza]

forehead	чело (с)	[tʃeló]
temple	слепоочие (с)	[slepoótʃie]
ear	ухо (с)	[uhó]
back of the head	тил (м)	[til]
neck	шия (ж)	[ʃíja]
throat	гърло (с)	[gə́rlo]

hair	коса (ж)	[kosá]
hairstyle	прическа (ж)	[pritʃéska]
haircut	подстригване (с)	[potstrígvane]
wig	перука (ж)	[perúka]

mustache	мустаци (м мн)	[mustátsi]
beard	брада (ж)	[bradá]
to have (a beard, etc.)	нося	[nósʲa]
braid	коса (ж)	[kosá]
sideburns	бакенбарди (мн)	[bakenbárdi]

| red-haired (adj) | червенокос | [tʃervenokós] |
| gray (hair) | беловлас | [belovlás] |

| bald (adj) | плешив | [pleʃív] |
| bald patch | плешивина (ж) | [pleʃiviná] |

| ponytail | опашка (ж) | [opáʃka] |
| bangs | бретон (м) | [bretón] |

62. Human body

| hand | китка (ж) | [kítka] |
| arm | ръка (ж) | [rəká] |

finger	пръст (м)	[prəst]
toe	пръст (м) на крак	[prəst na krak]
thumb	палец (м)	[pálets]
little finger	кутре (с)	[kutré]
nail	нокът (м)	[nókət]

fist	юмрук (м)	[jumrúk]
palm	длан (ж)	[dlan]
wrist	китка (ж)	[kítka]
forearm	предмишница (ж)	[predmíʃnitsa]
elbow	лакът (м)	[lákət]
shoulder	рамо (с)	[rámo]

leg	крак (м)	[krak]
foot	ходило (с)	[hodílo]
knee	коляно (с)	[kolʲáno]
calf (part of leg)	прасец (м)	[praséts]
hip	бедро (с)	[bedró]
heel	пета (ж)	[petá]

body	тяло (с)	[tʲálo]
stomach	корем (м)	[korém]
chest	гръд (ж)	[grəd]
breast	женска гръд (ж)	[ʒénska grəd]
flank	страна (ж)	[straná]
back	гръб (м)	[grəp]

| lower back | кръст (м) | [krəst] |
| waist | талия (ж) | [tálija] |

navel (belly button)	пъп (м)	[pəp]
buttocks	седалище (с)	[sedáliʃte]
bottom	задник (м)	[zádnik]

beauty mark	бенка (ж)	[bénka]
birthmark	родилно петно (с)	[rodílno petnó]
(café au lait spot)		
tattoo	татуировка (ж)	[tatuirófka]
scar	белег (м)	[bélek]

63. Diseases

sickness	болест (ж)	[bólest]
to be sick	боледувам	[boledúvam]
health	здраве (с)	[zdráve]
runny nose (coryza)	хрема (ж)	[hréma]
tonsillitis	ангина (ж)	[angína]
cold (illness)	настинка (ж)	[nastínka]
to catch a cold	настина	[nastína]
bronchitis	бронхит (м)	[bronhít]
pneumonia	пневмония (ж)	[pnevmoníja]
flu, influenza	грип (м)	[grip]
nearsighted (adj)	късоглед	[kəsoglét]
farsighted (adj)	далекоглед	[dalekoglét]
strabismus (crossed eyes)	кривогледство (с)	[krivoglétstvo]
cross-eyed (adj)	кривоглед	[krivoglét]
cataract	катаракта (ж)	[katarákta]
glaucoma	глаукома (ж)	[glaukóma]
stroke	инсулт (м)	[insúlt]
heart attack	инфаркт (м)	[infárkt]
myocardial infarction	инфаркт (м) на миокарда	[infárkt na miokárda]
paralysis	парализа (ж)	[paráliza]
to paralyze (vt)	парализирам	[paralizíram]
allergy	алергия (ж)	[alérgija]
asthma	астма (ж)	[ástma]
diabetes	диабет (м)	[diabét]
toothache	зъбобол (м)	[zəboból]
caries	кариес (м)	[káries]
diarrhea	диария (ж)	[diárija]
constipation	запек (м)	[zápek]
stomach upset	разстройство (с) на стомаха	[rastrójstvo na stomáha]
food poisoning	отравяне (с)	[otrávʲane]
to get food poisoning	отровя се	[otróvʲa se]
arthritis	артрит (м)	[artrít]
rickets	рахит (м)	[rahít]
rheumatism	ревматизъм (м)	[revmatízəm]
atherosclerosis	атеросклероза (ж)	[ateroskleróza]
gastritis	гастрит (м)	[gastrít]
appendicitis	апандисит (м)	[apandisít]
cholecystitis	холецистит (м)	[holetsistít]

ulcer	язва (ж)	[jázva]
measles	дребна шарка (ж)	[drébna ʃárka]
rubella (German measles)	шарка (ж)	[ʃárka]
jaundice	жълтеница (ж)	[ʒəltenítsa]
hepatitis	хепатит (м)	[hepatít]

schizophrenia	шизофрения (ж)	[ʃizofreníja]
rabies (hydrophobia)	бяс (м)	[bʲas]
neurosis	невроза (ж)	[nevróza]
concussion	сътресение (с) на мозъка	[sətresénie na mózəka]

cancer	рак (м)	[rak]
sclerosis	склероза (ж)	[skleróza]
multiple sclerosis	множествена склероза (ж)	[mnóʒestvena skleróza]

alcoholism	алкохолизъм (м)	[alkoholízəm]
alcoholic (n)	алкохолик (м)	[alkoholík]
syphilis	сифилис (м)	[sífilis]
AIDS	СПИН (м)	[spin]

tumor	тумор (м)	[túmor]
malignant (adj)	злокачествен	[zlokátʃestven]
benign (adj)	доброкачествен	[dobrokátʃestven]

fever	треска (ж)	[tréska]
malaria	малария (ж)	[malárija]
gangrene	гангрена (ж)	[gangréna]
seasickness	морска болест (ж)	[mórska bólest]
epilepsy	епилепсия (ж)	[epilépsija]

epidemic	епидемия (ж)	[epidémija]
typhus	тиф (м)	[tif]
tuberculosis	туберкулоза (ж)	[tuberkulóza]
cholera	холера (ж)	[holéra]
plague (bubonic ~)	чума (ж)	[tʃúma]

64. Symptoms. Treatments. Part 1

symptom	симптом (м)	[simptóm]
temperature	температура (ж)	[temperatúra]
high temperature (fever)	висока температура (ж)	[visóka temperatúra]
pulse (heartbeat)	пулс (м)	[puls]

dizziness (vertigo)	световъртеж (м)	[svetovərtéʃ]
hot (adj)	горещ	[goréʃt]
shivering	тръпки (ж мн)	[trépki]
pale (e.g., ~ face)	бледен	[bléden]
cough	кашлица (ж)	[káʃlitsa]

to cough (vi)	кашлям	[káʃlam]
to sneeze (vi)	кихам	[kíham]
faint	припадък (м)	[pripádək]
to faint (vi)	припадна	[pripádna]
bruise (hématome)	синина (ж)	[sininá]
bump (lump)	подутина (ж)	[podutiná]
to bang (bump)	ударя се	[udárʲa se]
contusion (bruise)	натъртване (с)	[natə́rtvane]
to get a bruise	ударя се	[udárʲa se]
to limp (vi)	куцам	[kútsam]
dislocation	изкълчване (с)	[iskə́ltʃvane]
to dislocate (vt)	навехна	[navéhna]
fracture	фрактура (ж)	[fraktúra]
to have a fracture	счупя	[stʃúpʲa]
cut (e.g., paper ~)	порязване (с)	[porʲázvane]
to cut oneself	порежа се	[poréʒa se]
bleeding	кръвотечение (с)	[krəvotetʃénie]
burn (injury)	изгаряне (с)	[izgárʲane]
to get burned	опаря се	[opárʲa se]
to prick (vt)	бодна	[bódna]
to prick oneself	убода се	[ubodá se]
to injure (vt)	нараня	[naranʲá]
injury	рана (ж)	[rána]
wound	рана (ж)	[rána]
trauma	травма (ж)	[trávma]
to be delirious	бълнувам	[bəlnúvam]
to stutter (vi)	заеквам	[zaékvam]
sunstroke	слънчев удар (м)	[slóntʃev údar]

65. Symptoms. Treatments. Part 2

pain, ache	болка (ж)	[bólka]
splinter (in foot, etc.)	трънче (с)	[trántʃe]
sweat (perspiration)	пот (ж)	[pot]
to sweat (perspire)	потя се	[potʲá se]
vomiting	повръщане (с)	[povrə́ʃtane]
convulsions	гърчове (м мн)	[gártʃove]
pregnant (adj)	бременна	[brémenna]
to be born	родя се	[rodʲá se]
delivery, labor	раждане (с)	[ráʒdane]
to deliver (~ a baby)	раждам	[ráʒdam]
abortion	аборт (м)	[abórt]

breathing, respiration	дишане (c)	[díʃane]
in-breath (inhalation)	вдишване (c)	[vdíʃvane]
out-breath (exhalation)	издишване (c)	[izdíʃvane]
to exhale (breathe out)	издишам	[izdíʃam]
to inhale (vi)	направя вдишване	[naprávʲa vdíʃvane]

disabled person	инвалид (м)	[invalít]
cripple	сакат човек (м)	[sakát ʧovék]
drug addict	наркоман (м)	[narkomán]

deaf (adj)	глух	[gluh]
mute (adj)	ням	[nʲam]
deaf mute (adj)	глухоням	[gluhonʲám]

mad, insane (adj)	луд	[lut]
madman (demented person)	луд (м)	[lut]
madwoman	луда (ж)	[lúda]
to go insane	полудея	[poludéja]

gene	ген (м)	[gen]
immunity	имунитет (м)	[imunitét]
hereditary (adj)	наследствен	[naslétstven]
congenital (adj)	вроден	[vrodén]

virus	вирус (м)	[vírus]
microbe	микроб (м)	[mikróp]
bacterium	бактерия (ж)	[baktérija]
infection	инфекция (ж)	[inféktsija]

66. Symptoms. Treatments. Part 3

| hospital | болница (ж) | [bólnitsa] |
| patient | пациент (м) | [patsiént] |

diagnosis	диагноза (ж)	[diagnóza]
cure	лекуване (c)	[lekúvane]
medical treatment	лекуване (c)	[lekúvane]
to get treatment	лекувам се	[lekúvam se]
to treat (~ a patient)	лекувам	[lekúvam]
to nurse (look after)	грижа се	[gríʒa se]
care (nursing ~)	грижа (ж)	[gríʒa]

operation, surgery	операция (ж)	[operátsija]
to bandage (head, limb)	превържа	[prevérʒa]
bandaging	превързване (c)	[prevérzvane]

vaccination	ваксиниране (c)	[vaksinírane]
to vaccinate (vt)	ваксинирам	[vaksiníram]
injection, shot	инжекция (ж)	[inʒéktsija]

to give an injection	инжектирам	[inʒektíram]
attack	пристъп, припáдък (м)	[prístəp], [pripadək]
amputation	ампутация (ж)	[amputátsija]
to amputate (vt)	ампутирам	[amputíram]
coma	кома (ж)	[kóma]
to be in a coma	намирам се в кома	[namíram se v kóma]
intensive care	реанимация (ж)	[reanimátsija]

to recover (~ from flu)	оздравявам	[ozdravʲávam]
condition (patient's ~)	състояние (с)	[səstojánie]
consciousness	съзнание (с)	[səznánie]
memory (faculty)	памет (ж)	[pámet]

to pull out (tooth)	вадя	[vádʲa]
filling	пломба (ж)	[plómba]
to fill (a tooth)	пломбирам	[plombíram]

| hypnosis | хипноза (ж) | [hipnóza] |
| to hypnotize (vt) | хипнотизирам | [hipnotizíram] |

67. Medicine. Drugs. Accessories

medicine, drug	лекарство (с)	[lekárstvo]
remedy	средство (с)	[srétstvo]
to prescribe (vt)	предпиша	[pretpíʃa]
prescription	рецепта (ж)	[retsépta]

tablet, pill	таблетка (ж)	[tablétka]
ointment	мехлем (м)	[mehlém]
ampule	ампула (ж)	[ampúla]
mixture, solution	микстура (ж)	[mikstúra]
syrup	сироп (м)	[siróp]
capsule	хапче (с)	[háptʃe]
powder	прах (м)	[prah]

gauze bandage	бинт (м)	[bint]
cotton wool	памук (м)	[pamúk]
iodine	йод (м)	[jot]

Band-Aid	пластир (м)	[plastír]
eyedropper	капкомер (м)	[kapkomér]
thermometer	термометър (м)	[termométər]
syringe	спринцовка (ж)	[sprintsófka]

| wheelchair | инвалидна количка (ж) | [invalídna kolítʃka] |
| crutches | патерици (ж мн) | [páteritsi] |

| painkiller | обезболяващо средство (с) | [obezbolʲávaʃto srétstvo] |
| laxative | очистително (с) | [otʃistítelno] |

spirits (ethanol)	**спирт** (м)	[spirt]
medicinal herbs	**билка** (ж)	[bílka]
herbal (~ tea)	**билков**	[bílkov]

T&P BOOKS

APARTMENT

T&P Books Publishing

68. Apartment

apartment	апартамент (м)	[apartamént]
room	стая (ж)	[stája]
bedroom	спалня (ж)	[spálnʲa]
dining room	столова (ж)	[stolová]
living room	гостна (ж)	[góstna]
study (home office)	кабинет (м)	[kabinét]
entry room	антре (с)	[antré]
bathroom (room with a bath or shower)	баня (ж)	[bánʲa]
half bath	тоалетна (ж)	[toalétna]
ceiling	таван (м)	[taván]
floor	под (м)	[pot]
corner	ъгъл (м)	[ə́gəl]

69. Furniture. Interior

furniture	мебели (мн)	[mébeli]
table	маса (ж)	[mása]
chair	стол (м)	[stol]
bed	легло (с)	[legló]
couch, sofa	диван (м)	[diván]
armchair	фотьойл (м)	[fotʲójl]
bookcase	книжен шкаф (м)	[kníʒen ʃkaf]
shelf	рафт (м)	[raft]
wardrobe	гардероб (м)	[garderóp]
coat rack (wall-mounted ~)	закачалка (ж)	[zakatʃálka]
coat stand	закачалка (ж)	[zakatʃálka]
bureau, dresser	скрин (м)	[skrin]
coffee table	малка масичка (ж)	[málka másitʃka]
mirror	огледало (с)	[ogledálo]
carpet	килим (м)	[kilím]
rug, small carpet	килимче (с)	[kilímtʃe]
fireplace	камина (ж)	[kamína]
candle	свещ (м)	[sveʃt]
candlestick	свещник (м)	[svéʃtnik]

drapes	пердета (с мн)	[perdéta]
wallpaper	тапети (м мн)	[tapéti]
blinds (jalousie)	щора (ж)	[ʃtóra]

table lamp	лампа (ж) за маса	[lámpa za mása]
wall lamp (sconce)	светилник (м)	[svetílnik]
floor lamp	лампион (м)	[lampión]
chandelier	полилей (м)	[poliléj]

leg (of chair, table)	крак (м)	[krak]
armrest	подлакътник (м)	[podlákətnik]
back (backrest)	облегалка (ж)	[oblegálka]
drawer	чекмедже (с)	[tʃekmedʒé]

70. Bedding

bedclothes	спално бельо (с)	[spálno belʲó]
pillow	възглавница (ж)	[vezglávnitsa]
pillowcase	калъфка (ж)	[kaléfka]
duvet, comforter	одеяло (с)	[odejálo]
sheet	чаршаф (м)	[tʃarʃáf]
bedspread	завивка (ж)	[zavífka]

71. Kitchen

kitchen	кухня (ж)	[kúhnʲa]
gas	газ (м)	[gas]
gas stove (range)	газова печка (ж)	[gázova pétʃka]
electric stove	електрическа печка (ж)	[elektrítʃeska pétʃka]
oven	фурна (ж)	[fúrna]
microwave oven	микровълнова печка (ж)	[mikrovélnova pétʃka]

refrigerator	хладилник (м)	[hladílnik]
freezer	фризер (м)	[frízer]
dishwasher	съдомиялна машина (ж)	[sədomijálna maʃína]

meat grinder	месомелачка (ж)	[meso·melátʃka]
juicer	сокоизстисквачка (ж)	[soko·isstiskvátʃka]
toaster	тостер (м)	[tóster]
mixer	миксер (м)	[míkser]

coffee machine	кафеварка (ж)	[kafevárka]
coffee pot	кафеник (м)	[kafeník]
coffee grinder	кафемелачка (ж)	[kafe·melátʃka]

kettle	чайник (м)	[tʃájnik]
teapot	чайник (м)	[tʃájnik]
lid	капачка (ж)	[kapátʃka]

tea strainer	цедка (ж)	[tsétka]
spoon	лъжица (ж)	[ləʒítsa]
teaspoon	чаена лъжица (ж)	[ʧáena ləʒítsa]
soup spoon	супена лъжица (ж)	[súpena ləʒítsa]
fork	вилица (ж)	[vílitsa]
knife	нож (м)	[noʒ]
tableware (dishes)	съдове (м мн)	[sédove]
plate (dinner ~)	чиния (ж)	[ʧiníja]
saucer	малка чинийка (ж)	[málka ʧiníjka]
shot glass	чашка (ж)	[ʧáʃka]
glass (tumbler)	чаша (ж)	[ʧáʃa]
cup	чаша (ж)	[ʧáʃa]
sugar bowl	захарница (ж)	[zaharnítsa]
salt shaker	солница (ж)	[solnítsa]
pepper shaker	пиперница (ж)	[pipérnitsa]
butter dish	съд (м) за краве масло	[sət za kráve masló]
stock pot (soup pot)	тенджера (ж)	[téndʒera]
frying pan (skillet)	тиган (м)	[tigán]
ladle	черпак (м)	[ʧerpák]
colander	гевгир (м)	[gevgír]
tray (serving ~)	табла (ж)	[tábla]
bottle	бутилка (ж)	[butílka]
jar (glass)	буркан (м)	[burkán]
can	тенекия (ж)	[tenekíja]
bottle opener	отварачка (ж)	[otvaráʧka]
can opener	отварачка (ж)	[otvaráʧka]
corkscrew	тирбушон (м)	[tirbuʃón]
filter	филтър (м)	[fíltər]
to filter (vt)	филтрирам	[filtríram]
trash, garbage (food waste, etc.)	боклук (м)	[boklúk]
trash can (kitchen ~)	кофа (ж) за боклук	[kófa za boklúk]

72. Bathroom

bathroom	баня (ж)	[bánʲa]
water	вода (ж)	[vodá]
faucet	смесител (м)	[smesítel]
hot water	топла вода (ж)	[tópla vodá]
cold water	студена вода (ж)	[studéna vodá]
toothpaste	паста (ж) за зъби	[pásta za zébi]
to brush one's teeth	мия си зъбите	[míja si zébite]

toothbrush	четка (ж) за зъби	[ʧétka za zébi]
to shave (vi)	бръсна се	[brésna se]
shaving foam	пяна (ж) за бръснене	[pʲána za brésnene]
razor	бръснач (м)	[brəsnáʧ]

to wash (one's hands, etc.)	мия	[míja]
to take a bath	мия се	[míja se]
shower	душ (м)	[duʃ]
to take a shower	вземам душ	[vzémam duʃ]

bathtub	вана (ж)	[vána]
toilet (toilet bowl)	тоалетна чиния (ж)	[toalétna ʧiníja]
sink (washbasin)	мивка (ж)	[mífka]

| soap | сапун (м) | [sapún] |
| soap dish | сапуниерка (ж) | [sapuniérka] |

sponge	гъба (ж)	[gə́ba]
shampoo	шампоан (м)	[ʃampoán]
towel	кърпа (ж)	[kérpa]
bathrobe	хавлиен халат (м)	[havlíen halát]

laundry (laundering)	пране (с)	[prané]
washing machine	перална машина (ж)	[perálna maʃína]
to do the laundry	пера	[perá]
laundry detergent	прах (м) за пране	[prah za prané]

73. Household appliances

TV set	телевизор (м)	[televízoɪ]
tape recorder	касетофон (м)	[kasetofón]
VCR (video recorder)	видео (с)	[vídeo]
radio	радиоприемник (м)	[radio·priémnik]
player (CD, MP3, etc.)	плейър (м)	[pléər]

video projector	прожекционен апарат (м)	[proʒektsiónen aparát]
home movie theater	домашно кино (с)	[domáʃno kíno]
DVD player	DVD плейър (м)	[dividí pléer]
amplifier	усилвател (м)	[usilvátel]
video game console	игрова приставка (ж)	[igrová pristáfka]

video camera	видеокамера (ж)	[video·kámera]
camera (photo)	фотоапарат (м)	[fotoaparát]
digital camera	цифров фотоапарат (м)	[tsífrov fotoaparát]

vacuum cleaner	прахосмукачка (ж)	[praho·smukáʧka]
iron (e.g., steam ~)	ютия (ж)	[jutíja]
ironing board	дъска (ж) за гладене	[dəská za gládene]
telephone	телефон (м)	[telefón]

cell phone	**мобилен телефон** (м)	[mobílen telefón]
typewriter	**пишеща машинка** (ж)	[píʃeʃta maʃínka]
sewing machine	**шевна машина** (ж)	[ʃévna maʃína]

microphone	**микрофон** (м)	[mikrofón]
headphones	**слушалки** (ж мн)	[sluʃálki]
remote control (TV)	**пулт** (м)	[pult]

CD, compact disc	**CD диск** (м)	[sidí disk]
cassette, tape	**касета** (ж)	[kaséta]
vinyl record	**плоча** (ж)	[plótʃa]

T&P BOOKS

THE EARTH. WEATHER

T&P Books Publishing

space	космос (м)	[kósmos]
space (as adj)	космически	[kosmítʃeski]
outer space	космическо пространство (с)	[kosmítʃesko prostránstvo]
world	свят (м)	[svʲat]
universe	вселена (ж)	[fseléna]
galaxy	галактика (ж)	[galáktika]
star	звезда (ж)	[zvezdá]
constellation	съзвездие (с)	[səzvézdie]
planet	планета (ж)	[planéta]
satellite	спътник (м)	[spǝ́tnik]
meteorite	метеорит (м)	[meteorít]
comet	комета (ж)	[kométa]
asteroid	астероид (м)	[asteroít]
orbit	орбита (ж)	[órbita]
to revolve (~ around the Earth)	въртя се	[vǝrtʲá se]
atmosphere	атмосфера (ж)	[atmosféra]
the Sun	Слънце	[slǝ́ntse]
solar system	Слънчева система (ж)	[slǝ́ntʃeva sistéma]
solar eclipse	слънчево затъмнение (с)	[slǝ́ntʃevo zatǝmnénie]
the Earth	Земя	[zemʲá]
the Moon	Луна	[luná]
Mars	Марс	[mars]
Venus	Венера	[venéra]
Jupiter	Юпитер	[júpiter]
Saturn	Сатурн	[satúrn]
Mercury	Меркурий	[merkúrij]
Uranus	Уран	[urán]
Neptune	Нептун	[neptún]
Pluto	Плутон	[plutón]
Milky Way	Млечен Път	[mlétʃen pǝt]
Great Bear (Ursa Major)	Голяма Мечка	[golʲáma métʃka]
North Star	Полярна Звезда	[polʲárna zvezdá]

Martian	марсианец (м)	[marsiánets]
extraterrestrial (n)	извънземен (м)	[izvənzémen]
alien	пришелец (м)	[priʃeléts]
flying saucer	летяща чиния (ж)	[letʲáʃta tʃiníja]

spaceship	космически кораб (м)	[kosmítʃeski kórap]
space station	орбитална станция (ж)	[orbitálna stántsija]
blast-off	старт (м)	[start]

engine	двигател (м)	[dvigátel]
nozzle	дюза (ж)	[dʲúza]
fuel	гориво (с)	[gorívo]

cockpit, flight deck	кабина (ж)	[kabína]
antenna	антена (ж)	[anténa]
porthole	илюминатор (м)	[ilʲuminátor]
solar panel	слънчева батерия (ж)	[slʲéntʃeva batérija]
spacesuit	скафандър (м)	[skafándər]

| weightlessness | безтегловност (ж) | [bestegkövnost] |
| oxygen | кислород (м) | [kislorót] |

| docking (in space) | свързване (с) | [svérzvane] |
| to dock (vi, vt) | свързвам се | [svérzvam se] |

observatory	обсерватория (ж)	[opservatórija]
telescope	телескоп (м)	[teleskóp]
to observe (vt)	наблюдавам	[nablʲudávam]
to explore (vt)	изследвам	[isslédvam]

75. The Earth

the Earth	Земя (ж)	[zemʲá]
the globe (the Earth)	земно кълбо (с)	[zémno kəlbó]
planet	планета (ж)	[planéta]

atmosphere	атмосфера (ж)	[atmosféra]
geography	география (ж)	[geográfija]
nature	природа (ж)	[priróda]

globe (table ~)	глобус (м)	[glóbus]
map	карта (ж)	[kárta]
atlas	атлас (м)	[atlás]

Europe	Европа	[evrópa]
Asia	Азия	[ázija]
Africa	Африка	[áfrika]
Australia	Австралия	[afstrálija]
America	Америка	[amérika]
North America	Северна Америка	[séverna amérika]

South America	Южна Америка	[júʒna amérika]
Antarctica	Антарктида	[antarktída]
the Arctic	Арктика	[árktika]

76. Cardinal directions

north	север (м)	[séver]
to the north	на север	[na séver]
in the north	на север	[na séver]
northern (adj)	северен	[séveren]

south	юг (м)	[juk]
to the south	на юг	[na juk]
in the south	на юг	[na juk]
southern (adj)	южен	[júʒen]

west	запад (м)	[zápat]
to the west	на запад	[na zápat]
in the west	на запад	[na zápat]
western (adj)	западен	[západen]

east	изток (м)	[ístok]
to the east	на изток	[na ístok]
in the east	на изток	[na ístok]
eastern (adj)	източен	[ístotʃen]

77. Sea. Ocean

sea	море (с)	[moré]
ocean	океан (м)	[okeán]
gulf (bay)	залив (м)	[zálif]
straits	пролив (м)	[próliv]

continent (mainland)	материк (м)	[materík]
island	остров (м)	[óstrov]
peninsula	полуостров (м)	[poluóstrov]
archipelago	архипелаг (м)	[arhipelák]

bay, cove	залив (м)	[zálif]
harbor	залив (м)	[zálif]
lagoon	лагуна (ж)	[lagúna]
cape	нос (м)	[nos]

atoll	атол (м)	[atól]
reef	риф (м)	[rif]
coral	корал (м)	[korál]
coral reef	коралов риф (м)	[korálov rif]
deep (adj)	дълбок	[dəlbók]

depth (deep water)	дълбочина (ж)	[dəlbotʃiná]
abyss	бездна (ж)	[bézna]
trench (e.g., Mariana ~)	падина (ж)	[padiná]

| current (Ocean ~) | течение (с) | [tetʃénie] |
| to surround (bathe) | мия | [míja] |

| shore | бряг (м) | [brʲak] |
| coast | крайбрежие (с) | [krajbréʒie] |

flow (flood tide)	прилив (м)	[príliv]
ebb (ebb tide)	отлив (м)	[ótliv]
shoal	плитчина (ж)	[plittʃiná]
bottom (~ of the sea)	дъно (с)	[dǝno]

wave	вълна (ж)	[vǝlná]
crest (~ of a wave)	гребен (м) на вълна	[grében na vǝlná]
spume (sea foam)	пяна (ж)	[pʲána]

storm (sea storm)	буря (ж)	[búrʲa]
hurricane	ураган (м)	[uragán]
tsunami	цунами (с)	[tsunámi]
calm (dead ~)	безветрие (с)	[bezvétrie]
quiet, calm (adj)	спокоен	[spokóen]

| pole | полюс (м) | [pólʲus] |
| polar (adj) | полярен | [polʲáren] |

latitude	ширина (ж)	[ʃiriná]
longitude	дължина (ж)	[dǝlʒiná]
parallel	паралел (ж)	[paralél]
equator	екватор (м)	[ekvátɔr]

sky	небе (с)	[nebé]
horizon	хоризонт (м)	[horizónt]
air	въздух (м)	[vázduh]

lighthouse	фар (м)	[far]
to dive (vi)	гмуркам се	[gmúrkam se]
to sink (ab. boat)	потъна	[poténa]
treasures	съкровища (с мн)	[sǝkróviʃta]

78. Seas' and Oceans' names

Atlantic Ocean	Атлантически океан	[atlantítʃeski okeán]
Indian Ocean	Индийски океан	[indíjski okeán]
Pacific Ocean	Тихи океан	[tíhi okeán]
Arctic Ocean	Северен Ледовит океан	[séveren ledovít okeán]
Black Sea	Черно море	[tʃérno moré]
Red Sea	Червено море	[tʃervéno moré]

| Yellow Sea | Жълто море | [ʒélto moré] |
| White Sea | Бяло море | [bʲálo moré] |

Caspian Sea	Каспийско море	[káspijsko moré]
Dead Sea	Мъртво море	[mértvo moré]
Mediterranean Sea	Средиземно море	[sredizémno moré]

| Aegean Sea | Егейско море | [egéjsko moré] |
| Adriatic Sea | Адриатическо море | [adriatítʃesko moré] |

Arabian Sea	Арабско море	[arápsko moré]
Sea of Japan	Японско море	[japónsko moré]
Bering Sea	Берингово море	[beríngovo moré]
South China Sea	Южнокитайско море	[juʒnokitájsko moré]

Coral Sea	Коралово море	[korálovo moré]
Tasman Sea	Тасманово море	[tasmánovo moré]
Caribbean Sea	Карибско море	[karíbsko moré]

| Barents Sea | Баренцово море | [baréntsovo moré] |
| Kara Sea | Карско море | [kárско moré] |

North Sea	Северно море	[séverno moré]
Baltic Sea	Балтийско море	[baltíjsko moré]
Norwegian Sea	Норвежко море	[norvéʃko moré]

79. Mountains

mountain	планина (ж)	[planiná]
mountain range	планинска верига (ж)	[planínska veríga]
mountain ridge	планински хребет (м)	[planínski hrebét]

summit, top	връх (м)	[vrəh]
peak	пик (м)	[pik]
foot (~ of the mountain)	подножие (с)	[podnóʒie]
slope (mountainside)	склон (м)	[sklon]

volcano	вулкан (м)	[vulkán]
active volcano	действащ вулкан (м)	[déjstvaʃt vulkán]
dormant volcano	изгаснал вулкан (м)	[izgásnal vulkán]

eruption	изригване (с)	[izrígvane]
crater	кратер (м)	[kráter]
magma	магма (ж)	[mágma]
lava	лава (ж)	[láva]
molten (~ lava)	нажежен	[naʒeʒén]

canyon	каньон (м)	[kanjón]
gorge	дефиле (с)	[defilé]
crevice	тясна клисура (ж)	[tʲásna klisúra]

abyss (chasm)	пропаст (ж)	[própast]
pass, col	превал (м)	[prevál]
plateau	плато (с)	[pláto]
cliff	скала (ж)	[skalá]
hill	хълм (м)	[həlm]

glacier	ледник (м)	[lédnik]
waterfall	водопад (м)	[vodopát]
geyser	гейзер (м)	[géjzer]
lake	езеро (с)	[ézero]

plain	равнина (ж)	[ravniná]
landscape	пейзаж (м)	[pejzáʒ]
echo	ехо (с)	[ého]

alpinist	алпинист (м)	[alpiníst]
rock climber	катерач (м)	[katerátʃ]
to conquer (in climbing)	покорявам	[pokorʲávam]
climb (an easy ~)	възкачване (с)	[vəskátʃvane]

80. Mountains names

The Alps	Алпи	[álpi]
Mont Blanc	Мон Блан	[mon blan]
The Pyrenees	Пиринеи	[pirinéi]

The Carpathians	Карпати	[karpáti]
The Ural Mountains	Урал	[urál]
The Caucasus Mountains	Кавказ	[kafkáz]
Mount Elbrus	Елбрус	[elbɪús]

The Altai Mountains	Алтай	[altáj]
The Tian Shan	Тяншан	[tʲanʃan]
The Pamir Mountains	Памир	[pamír]
The Himalayas	Хималаи	[himalái]
Mount Everest	Еверест	[everést]

| The Andes | Анди | [ándi] |
| Mount Kilimanjaro | Килиманджаро | [kilimandʒáro] |

81. Rivers

river	река (ж)	[reká]
spring (natural source)	извор (м)	[ízvor]
riverbed (river channel)	корито (с)	[koríto]
basin (river valley)	басейн (м)	[baséjn]
to flow into …	вливам се	[vlívam se]
tributary	приток (м)	[prítok]

bank (of river)	бряг (м)	[brʲak]
current (stream)	течение (с)	[tetʃénie]
downstream (adv)	надолу по течението	[nadólu po tetʃénieto]
upstream (adv)	нагоре по течението	[nagóre po tetʃénieto]
inundation	наводнение (с)	[navodnénie]
flooding	пролетно пълноводие (с)	[prolétno pəlnovódie]
to overflow (vi)	разливам се	[razlívam se]
to flood (vt)	потопявам	[potopʲávam]
shallow (shoal)	плитчина (ж)	[plittʃiná]
rapids	праг (м)	[prak]
dam	яз (м)	[jaz]
canal	канал (м)	[kanál]
reservoir (artificial lake)	водохранилище (с)	[vodohranílifte]
sluice, lock	шлюз (м)	[ʃlʲuz]
water body (pond, etc.)	водоем (м)	[vodoém]
swamp (marshland)	блато (с)	[bláto]
bog, marsh	тресавище (с)	[tresávifte]
whirlpool	водовъртеж (м)	[vodovərtéʒ]
stream (brook)	ручей (м)	[rútʃej]
drinking (ab. water)	питеен	[pitéen]
fresh (~ water)	сладководен	[slatkovóden]
ice	лед (м)	[let]
to freeze over (ab. river, etc.)	замръзна	[zamrézna]

82. Rivers' names

Seine	Сена	[séna]
Loire	Лоара	[loára]
Thames	Темза	[témza]
Rhine	Рейн	[rejn]
Danube	Дунав	[dúnav]
Volga	Волга	[vólga]
Don	Дон	[don]
Lena	Лена	[léna]
Yellow River	Хуанхъ	[huanhé]
Yangtze	Яндзъ	[jandzé]
Mekong	Меконг	[mekónk]
Ganges	Ганг	[gang]
Nile River	Нил	[nil]

Congo River	Конго	[kóngo]
Okavango River	Окаванго	[okavángo]
Zambezi River	Замбези	[zambézi]
Limpopo River	Лимпопо	[limpopó]
Mississippi River	Мисисипи	[misisípi]

83. Forest

| forest, wood | гора (ж) | [gorá] |
| forest (as adj) | горски | [górski] |

thick forest	гъсталак (м)	[gəstalák]
grove	горичка (ж)	[gorítʃka]
forest clearing	поляна (ж)	[polʲána]

| thicket | гъсталак (м) | [gəstalák] |
| scrubland | храсталак (м) | [hrastalák] |

| footpath (troddenpath) | пътечка (ж) | [pətétʃka] |
| gully | овраг (м) | [ovrák] |

tree	дърво (с)	[dərvó]
leaf	лист (м)	[list]
leaves (foliage)	шума (ж)	[ʃúma]

fall of leaves	листопад (м)	[listopát]
to fall (ab. leaves)	опадвам	[opádvam]
top (of the tree)	връх (м)	[vrəh]

branch	клонка (м)	[klónka]
bough	дебел клон (м)	[debél klon]
bud (on shrub, tree)	пъпка (ж)	[pépka]
needle (of pine tree)	игла (ж)	[iglá]
pine cone	шишарка (ж)	[ʃiʃárka]

tree hollow	хралупа (ж)	[hralúpa]
nest	гнездо (с)	[gnezdó]
burrow (animal hole)	дупка (ж)	[dúpka]

trunk	стъбло (с)	[stəbló]
root	корен (м)	[kóren]
bark	кора (ж)	[korá]
moss	мъх (м)	[məh]

to uproot (remove trees or tree stumps)	изкоренявам	[izkorenʲávam]
to chop down	сека	[seká]
to deforest (vt)	изсичам	[issítʃam]
tree stump	пън (м)	[pən]
campfire	клада (ж)	[kláda]

| forest fire | пожар (м) | [poʒár] |
| to extinguish (vt) | загасявам | [zagasʲávam] |

forest ranger	горски пазач (м)	[górski pazátʃ]
protection	опазване (с)	[opázvane]
to protect (~ nature)	опазвам	[opázvam]
poacher	бракониер (м)	[brakoniér]
steel trap	капан (м)	[kapán]

| to gather, to pick (vt) | събирам | [səbíram] |
| to lose one's way | загубя се | [zagúbʲa se] |

84. Natural resources

natural resources	природни ресурси (м мн)	[priródni resúrsi]
minerals	полезни изкопаеми (с мн)	[polézni iskopáemi]
deposits	залежи (мн)	[zaléʒi]
field (e.g., oilfield)	находище (с)	[nahódiʃte]

to mine (extract)	добивам	[dobívam]
mining (extraction)	добиване (с)	[dobívane]
ore	руда (ж)	[rudá]
mine (e.g., for coal)	рудник (м)	[rúdnik]
shaft (mine ~)	шахта (ж)	[ʃáhta]
miner	миньор (м)	[minʲór]

| gas (natural ~) | газ (м) | [gas] |
| gas pipeline | газопровод (м) | [gazoprovót] |

oil (petroleum)	нефт (м)	[neft]
oil pipeline	нефтопровод (м)	[neftoprovót]
oil well	нефтена кула (ж)	[néftena kúla]
derrick (tower)	сондажна кула (ж)	[sondáʒna kúla]
tanker	танкер (м)	[tánker]

sand	пясък (м)	[pʲásək]
limestone	варовик (м)	[varóvik]
gravel	дребен чакъл (м)	[drében tʃakél]
peat	торф (м)	[torf]
clay	глина (ж)	[glína]
coal	въглища (мн)	[végliʃta]

iron (ore)	желязо (с)	[ʒelʲázo]
gold	злато (с)	[zláto]
silver	сребро (с)	[srebró]
nickel	никел (м)	[níkel]
copper	мед (ж)	[met]
zinc	цинк (м)	[tsink]
manganese	манган (м)	[mangán]

| mercury | живак (м) | [ʒivák] |
| lead | олово (с) | [olóvo] |

mineral	минерал (м)	[minerál]
crystal	кристал (м)	[kristál]
marble	мрамор (м)	[mrámor]
uranium	уран (м)	[urán]

85. Weather

weather	време (с)	[vréme]
weather forecast	прогноза (ж) за времето	[prognóza za vrémeto]
temperature	температура (ж)	[temperatúra]
thermometer	термометър (м)	[termométər]
barometer	барометър (м)	[barométər]

humid (adj)	влажен	[vláʒen]
humidity	влажност (ж)	[vláʒnost]
heat (extreme ~)	пек (м)	[pek]
hot (torrid)	горещ	[goréʃt]
it's hot	горещо	[goréʃto]

| it's warm | топло | [tóplo] |
| warm (moderately hot) | топъл | [tópəl] |

| it's cold | студено | [studéno] |
| cold (adj) | студен | [studén] |

sun	слънце (с)	[sléntse]
to shine (vi)	грея	[gréjа]
sunny (day)	слънчев	[sléntʃev]
to come up (vi)	изгрея	[izgréja]
to set (vi)	заляза	[zalʲáza]

cloud	облак (м)	[óblak]
cloudy (adj)	облачен	[óblatʃen]
rain cloud	голям облак (м)	[golʲám óblak]
somber (gloomy)	навъсен	[navésen]

rain	дъжд (м)	[dəʒt]
it's raining	вали дъжд	[valí dəʒt]
rainy (~ day, weather)	дъждовен	[dəʒdóven]
to drizzle (vi)	ръмя	[rəmʲá]

pouring rain	пороен дъжд (м)	[poróen dəʒt]
downpour	порой (м)	[porój]
heavy (e.g., ~ rain)	силен	[sílen]
puddle	локва (ж)	[lókva]
to get wet (in rain)	намокря се	[namókrʲa se]
fog (mist)	мъгла (ж)	[məglá]

foggy	мъглив	[məglíf]
snow	сняг (м)	[snʲak]
it's snowing	вали сняг	[valí snʲak]

86. Severe weather. Natural disasters

thunderstorm	гръмотевична буря (ж)	[grəmotévitʃna búrʲa]
lightning (~ strike)	мълния (ж)	[mélnija]
to flash (vi)	блясвам	[blʲásvam]

thunder	гръм (м)	[grəm]
to thunder (vi)	гърмя	[gərmʲá]
it's thundering	гърми	[gərmí]

| hail | градушка (ж) | [gradúʃka] |
| it's hailing | пада градушка | [páda gradúʃka] |

| to flood (vt) | потопя | [potopʲá] |
| flood, inundation | наводнение (с) | [navodnénie] |

earthquake	земетресение (с)	[zemetresénie]
tremor, shoke	трус (м)	[trus]
epicenter	епицентър (м)	[epitséntər]

| eruption | изригване (с) | [izrígvane] |
| lava | лава (ж) | [láva] |

| twister, tornado | торнадо (с) | [tornádo] |
| typhoon | тайфун (м) | [tajfún] |

hurricane	ураган (м)	[uragán]
storm	буря (ж)	[búrʲa]
tsunami	цунами (с)	[tsunámi]

cyclone	циклон (м)	[tsiklón]
bad weather	лошо време (с)	[lóʃo vréme]
fire (accident)	пожар (м)	[poʒár]
disaster	катастрофа (ж)	[katastrófa]
meteorite	метеорит (м)	[meteorít]

avalanche	лавина (ж)	[lavína]
snowslide	лавина (ж)	[lavína]
blizzard	виелица (ж)	[viélitsa]
snowstorm	снежна буря (ж)	[snéʒna búrʲa]

FAUNA

T&P Books Publishing

87. Mammals. Predators

predator	**хищник** (м)	[híʃtnik]
tiger	**тигър** (м)	[tígər]
lion	**лъв** (м)	[ləv]
wolf	**вълк** (м)	[vəlk]
fox	**лисица** (ж)	[lisítsa]
jaguar	**ягуар** (м)	[jaguár]
leopard	**леопард** (м)	[leopárt]
cheetah	**гепард** (м)	[gepárt]
black panther	**пантера** (ж)	[pantéra]
puma	**пума** (ж)	[púma]
snow leopard	**снежен барс** (м)	[snéʒen bars]
lynx	**рис** (м)	[ris]
coyote	**койот** (м)	[kojót]
jackal	**чакал** (м)	[tʃakál]
hyena	**хиена** (ж)	[hiéna]

88. Wild animals

animal	**животно** (с)	[ʒivótno]
beast (animal)	**звяр** (м)	[zvʲar]
squirrel	**катерица** (ж)	[káteritsa]
hedgehog	**таралеж** (м)	[taraléʒ]
hare	**заек** (м)	[záek]
rabbit	**питомен заек** (м)	[pítomen záek]
badger	**язовец** (м)	[jázovets]
raccoon	**енот** (м)	[enót]
hamster	**хамстер** (м)	[hámster]
marmot	**мармот** (м)	[marmót]
mole	**къртица** (ж)	[kərtítsa]
mouse	**мишка** (ж)	[míʃka]
rat	**плъх** (м)	[pləh]
bat	**прилеп** (м)	[prílep]
ermine	**хермелин** (м)	[hermelín]
sable	**самур** (м)	[samúr]
marten	**бялка** (ж)	[bʲálka]

| weasel | невестулка (ж) | [nevestúlka] |
| mink | норка (ж) | [nórka] |

| beaver | бобър (м) | [bóbər] |
| otter | видра (ж) | [vídra] |

horse	кон (м)	[kon]
moose	лос (м)	[los]
deer	елен (м)	[elén]
camel	камила (ж)	[kamíla]

bison	бизон (м)	[bizón]
wisent	зубър (м)	[zúbər]
buffalo	бивол (м)	[bívol]

zebra	зебра (ж)	[zébra]
antelope	антилопа (ж)	[antilópa]
roe deer	сърна (ж)	[sərná]
fallow deer	лопатар (м)	[lopatár]
chamois	сърна (ж)	[sərná]
wild boar	глиган (м)	[gligán]

whale	кит (м)	[kit]
seal	тюлен (м)	[tʲulén]
walrus	морж (м)	[morʒ]
fur seal	морска котка (ж)	[mórska kótka]
dolphin	делфин (м)	[delfín]

bear	мечка (ж)	[métʃka]
polar bear	бяла мечка (ж)	[bʲála métʃka]
panda	панда (ж)	[pánda]

monkey	маймуна (ж)	[majmúna]
chimpanzee	шимпанзе (с)	[ʃimpanzé]
orangutan	орангутан (м)	[orangután]
gorilla	горила (ж)	[goríla]
macaque	макак (м)	[makák]
gibbon	гибон (м)	[gibón]

| elephant | слон (м) | [slon] |
| rhinoceros | носорог (м) | [nosorók] |

| giraffe | жираф (м) | [ʒiráf] |
| hippopotamus | хипопотам (м) | [hipopotám] |

| kangaroo | кенгуру (с) | [kénguru] |
| koala (bear) | коала (ж) | [koála] |

mongoose	мангуста (ж)	[mangústa]
chinchilla	чинчила (ж)	[tʃintʃíla]
skunk	скунс (м)	[skuns]
porcupine	бодливец (м)	[bodlívets]

89. Domestic animals

cat	котка (ж)	[kótka]
tomcat	котарак (м)	[kotarák]
horse	кон (м)	[kon]
stallion (male horse)	жребец (м)	[ʒrebéts]
mare	кобила (ж)	[kobíla]
cow	крава (ж)	[kráva]
bull	бик (м)	[bik]
ox	вол (м)	[vol]
sheep (ewe)	овца (ж)	[ovtsá]
ram	овен (м)	[ovén]
goat	коза (ж)	[kozá]
billy goat, he-goat	козел (м)	[kozél]
donkey	магаре (с)	[magáre]
mule	муле (с)	[múle]
pig, hog	свиня (ж)	[svinʲá]
piglet	прасе (с)	[prasé]
rabbit	питомен заек (м)	[pítomen záek]
hen (chicken)	кокошка (ж)	[kokóʃka]
rooster	петел (м)	[petél]
duck	патица (ж)	[pátitsa]
drake	паток (м)	[patók]
goose	гъсок (м)	[gəsók]
tom turkey, gobbler	пуяк (м)	[pújak]
turkey (hen)	пуйка (ж)	[pújka]
domestic animals	домашни животни (с мн)	[domáʃni ʒivótni]
tame (e.g., ~ hamster)	питомен	[pítomen]
to tame (vt)	опитомявам	[opitomʲávam]
to breed (vt)	отглеждам	[otgléʒdam]
farm	ферма (ж)	[férma]
poultry	домашна птица (ж)	[domáʃna ptítsa]
cattle	добитък (м)	[dobítək]
herd (cattle)	стадо (с)	[stádo]
stable	обор (м)	[obór]
pigpen	кочина (ж)	[kótʃina]
cowshed	краварник (м)	[kravárnik]
rabbit hutch	зайчарник (м)	[zajtʃárnik]
hen house	курник (м)	[kúrnik]

90. Birds

bird	птица (ж)	[ptítsa]
pigeon	гълъб (м)	[géləp]
sparrow	врабче (с)	[vrabʧé]
tit (great tit)	синигер (м)	[sinigér]
magpie	сврака (ж)	[svráka]
raven	гарван (м)	[gárvan]
crow	врана (ж)	[vrána]
jackdaw	гарга (ж)	[gárga]
rook	полски гарван (м)	[pólski gárvan]
duck	патица (ж)	[pátitsa]
goose	гъсок (м)	[gəsók]
pheasant	фазан (м)	[fazán]
eagle	орел (м)	[orél]
hawk	ястреб (м)	[jástrep]
falcon	сокол (м)	[sokól]
vulture	гриф (м)	[grif]
condor (Andean ~)	кондор (м)	[kondór]
swan	лебед (м)	[lébet]
crane	жерав (м)	[ʒérav]
stork	щъркел (м)	[ʃtérkel]
parrot	папагал (м)	[papagál]
hummingbird	колибри (с)	[kolíbri]
peacock	паун (м)	[paún]
ostrich	щраус (м)	[ʃtráus]
heron	чапла (ж)	[ʧápla]
flamingo	фламинго (с)	[flamíngo]
pelican	пеликан (м)	[pelikán]
nightingale	славей (м)	[slávej]
swallow	лястовица (ж)	[lʲástovitsa]
thrush	дрозд (м)	[drozd]
song thrush	поен дрозд (м)	[póen drozd]
blackbird	кос, черен дрозд (м)	[kos], [ʧéren drozd]
swift	бързолет (м)	[bərzolét]
lark	чучулига (ж)	[ʧuʧulíga]
quail	пъдпъдък (м)	[pədpədék]
woodpecker	кълвач (м)	[kəlváʧ]
cuckoo	кукувица (ж)	[kúkuvitsa]
owl	сова (ж)	[sóva]
eagle owl	бухал (м)	[búhal]

wood grouse	глухар (м)	[gluhár]
black grouse	тетрев (м)	[tétrev]
partridge	яребица (ж)	[járebitsa]

starling	скорец (м)	[skoréts]
canary	канарче (с)	[kanártʃe]
hazel grouse	лещарка (ж)	[leʃtárka]
chaffinch	чинка (ж)	[tʃínka]
bullfinch	червенушка (ж)	[tʃervenúʃka]

seagull	чайка (ж)	[tʃájka]
albatross	албатрос (м)	[albatrós]
penguin	пингвин (м)	[pingvín]

91. Fish. Marine animals

bream	платика (ж)	[platíka]
carp	шаран (м)	[ʃarán]
perch	костур (м)	[kostúr]
catfish	сом (м)	[som]
pike	щука (ж)	[ʃtúka]

| salmon | сьомга (ж) | [sʲómga] |
| sturgeon | есетра (ж) | [esétra] |

herring	селда (ж)	[sélda]
Atlantic salmon	сьомга (ж)	[sʲómga]
mackerel	скумрия (ж)	[skumríja]
flatfish	калкан (м)	[kalkán]

zander, pike perch	бяла риба (ж)	[bʲála ríba]
cod	треска (ж)	[tréska]
tuna	риба тон (м)	[ríba ton]
trout	пъстърва (ж)	[pəstérva]

eel	змиорка (ж)	[zmiórka]
electric ray	електрически скат (м)	[elektrítʃeski skat]
moray eel	мурена (ж)	[muréna]
piranha	пираня (ж)	[piránʲa]

shark	акула (ж)	[akúla]
dolphin	делфин (м)	[delfín]
whale	кит (м)	[kit]

crab	морски рак (м)	[mórski rak]
jellyfish	медуза (ж)	[medúza]
octopus	октопод (м)	[oktopót]

| starfish | морска звезда (ж) | [mórska zvezdá] |
| sea urchin | морски таралеж (м) | [mórski taraléʒ] |

seahorse	морско конче (c)	[mórsko kóntʃe]
oyster	стрида (ж)	[strída]
shrimp	скарида (ж)	[skarída]
lobster	омар (м)	[omár]
spiny lobster	лангуста (ж)	[langústa]

92. Amphibians. Reptiles

snake	змия (ж)	[zmijá]
venomous (snake)	отровен	[otróven]
viper	усойница (ж)	[usójnitsa]
cobra	кобра (ж)	[kóbra]
python	питон (м)	[pitón]
boa	боа (ж)	[boá]
grass snake	смок (м)	[smok]
rattle snake	гърмяща змия (ж)	[gərmʲáʃta zmijá]
anaconda	анаконда (ж)	[anakónda]
lizard	гущер (м)	[gúʃter]
iguana	игуана (ж)	[iguána]
monitor lizard	варан (м)	[varán]
salamander	саламандър (м)	[salamándər]
chameleon	хамелеон (м)	[hameleón]
scorpion	скорпион (м)	[skorpión]
turtle	костенурка (ж)	[kostenúrka]
frog	водна жаба (ж)	[vódna ʒába]
toad	жаба (ж)	[ʒába]
crocodile	крокодил (м)	[krokodíl]

93. Insects

insect, bug	насекомо (c)	[nasekómo]
butterfly	пеперуда (ж)	[peperúda]
ant	мравка (ж)	[mráfka]
fly	муха (ж)	[muhá]
mosquito	комар (м)	[komár]
beetle	бръмбар (м)	[brémbar]
wasp	оса (ж)	[osá]
bee	пчела (ж)	[ptʃelá]
bumblebee	земна пчела (ж)	[zémna ptʃelá]
gadfly (botfly)	щръклица (ж), овод (м)	[ʃtréklitsa], [óvot]
spider	паяк (м)	[pájak]
spiderweb	паяжина (ж)	[pájaʒina]

dragonfly	**водно конче** (с)	[vódno kóntʃe]
grasshopper	**скакалец** (м)	[skakaléts]
moth (night butterfly)	**нощна пеперуда** (ж)	[nóʃtna peperúda]
cockroach	**хлебарка** (ж)	[hlebárka]
tick	**кърлеж** (м)	[kárleʃ]
flea	**бълха** (ж)	[bəlhá]
midge	**мушица** (ж)	[muʃítsa]
locust	**прелетен скакалец** (м)	[préleten skakaléts]
snail	**охлюв** (м)	[óhlʲuf]
cricket	**щурец** (м)	[ʃturéts]
lightning bug	**светулка** (ж)	[svetúlka]
ladybug	**калинка** (ж)	[kalínka]
cockchafer	**майски бръмбар** (м)	[májski brémbar]
leech	**пиявица** (ж)	[pijávitsa]
caterpillar	**гъсеница** (ж)	[gəsénitsa]
earthworm	**червей** (м)	[tʃérvej]
larva	**буба** (ж)	[búba]

T&P BOOKS

FLORA

T&P Books Publishing

94. Trees

tree	дърво (с)	[dərvó]
deciduous (adj)	широколистно	[ʃirokolístno]
coniferous (adj)	иглолистно	[iglolístno]
evergreen (adj)	вечнозелено	[vetʃnozeléno]
apple tree	ябълка (ж)	[jábəlka]
pear tree	круша (ж)	[krúʃa]
sweet cherry tree	череша (ж)	[tʃeréʃa]
sour cherry tree	вишна (ж)	[víʃna]
plum tree	слива (ж)	[slíva]
birch	бреза (ж)	[brezá]
oak	дъб (м)	[dəp]
linden tree	липа (ж)	[lipá]
aspen	трепетлика (ж)	[trepetlíka]
maple	клен (м)	[klen]
spruce	ела (ж)	[elá]
pine	бор (м)	[bor]
larch	лиственица (ж)	[lístvenitsa]
fir tree	бяла ела (ж)	[bʲála elá]
cedar	кедър (м)	[kédər]
poplar	топола (ж)	[topóla]
rowan	офика (ж)	[ofíka]
willow	върба (ж)	[vərbá]
alder	елша (ж)	[elʃá]
beech	бук (м)	[buk]
elm	бряст (м)	[brʲast]
ash (tree)	ясен (м)	[jásen]
chestnut	кестен (м)	[késten]
magnolia	магнолия (ж)	[magnólija]
palm tree	палма (ж)	[pálma]
cypress	кипарис (м)	[kiparís]
mangrove	мангрово дърво (с)	[mangrovo dərvó]
baobab	баобаб (м)	[baobáp]
eucalyptus	евкалипт (м)	[efkalípt]
sequoia	секвоя (ж)	[sekvója]

95. Shrubs

bush	храст (м)	[hrast]
shrub	храсталак (м)	[hrastalák]
grapevine	грозде (с)	[grózde]
vineyard	лозе (с)	[lóze]
raspberry bush	малина (ж)	[malína]
blackcurrant bush	черно френско грозде (с)	[tʃérno frénsko grózde]
redcurrant bush	червено френско грозде (с)	[tʃervéno frénsko grózde]
gooseberry bush	цариградско грозде (с)	[tsarigrátsko grózde]
acacia	акация (ж)	[akátsija]
barberry	кисел трън (м)	[kísel trən]
jasmine	жасмин (м)	[ʒasmín]
juniper	хвойна, смрика (ж)	[hvójna], [smríka]
rosebush	розов храст (м)	[rózov hrast]
dog rose	шипка (ж)	[ʃípka]

96. Fruits. Berries

fruit	плод (м)	[plot]
fruits	плодове (м мн)	[plodové]
apple	ябълка (ж)	[jábəlka]
pear	круша (ж)	[krúʃa]
plum	слива (ж)	[slíva]
strawberry (garden ~)	ягода (ж)	[jágoda]
sour cherry	вишна (ж)	[víʃna]
sweet cherry	череша (ж)	[tʃeréʃa]
grape	грозде (с)	[grózde]
raspberry	малина (ж)	[malína]
blackcurrant	черно френско грозде (с)	[tʃérno frénsko grózde]
redcurrant	червено френско грозде (с)	[tʃervéno frénsko grózde]
gooseberry	цариградско грозде (с)	[tsarigrátsko grózde]
cranberry	клюква (ж)	[klʲúkva]
orange	портокал (м)	[portokál]
mandarin	мандарина (ж)	[mandarína]
pineapple	ананас (м)	[ananás]
banana	банан (м)	[banán]
date	фурма (ж)	[furmá]

lemon	лимон (м)	[limón]
apricot	кайсия (ж)	[kajsíja]
peach	праскова (ж)	[práskova]
kiwi	киви (с)	[kívi]
grapefruit	грейпфрут (м)	[gréjpfrut]

berry	горски плод (м)	[górski plot]
berries	горски плодове (м мн)	[górski plodové]
cowberry	червена боровинка (ж)	[tʃervéna borovínka]
wild strawberry	горска ягода (ж)	[górska jágoda]
bilberry	черна боровинка (ж)	[tʃérna borovínka]

97. Flowers. Plants

| flower | цвете (с) | [tsvéte] |
| bouquet (of flowers) | букет (м) | [bukét] |

rose (flower)	роза (ж)	[róza]
tulip	лале (с)	[lalé]
carnation	карамфил (м)	[karamfíl]
gladiolus	гладиола (ж)	[gladióla]

cornflower	метличина (ж)	[metlitʃína]
harebell	камбанка (ж)	[kambánka]
dandelion	глухарче (с)	[gluhártʃe]
camomile	лайка (ж)	[lájka]

aloe	алое (с)	[alóe]
cactus	кактус (м)	[káktus]
rubber plant, ficus	фикус (м)	[fíkus]

lily	лилиум (м)	[lílium]
geranium	мушкато (с)	[muʃkáto]
hyacinth	зюмбюл (м)	[zʲúmbʲúl]

mimosa	мимоза (ж)	[mimóza]
narcissus	нарцис (м)	[nartsís]
nasturtium	латинка (ж)	[latínka]

orchid	орхидея (ж)	[orhidéja]
peony	божур (м)	[boʒúr]
violet	теменуга (ж)	[temenúga]

pansy	трицветна теменуга (ж)	[tritsvétna temenúga]
forget-me-not	незабравка (ж)	[nezabráfka]
daisy	маргаритка (ж)	[margarítka]

poppy	мак (м)	[mak]
hemp	коноп (м)	[konóp]
mint	мента (ж)	[ménta]

| lily of the valley | момина сълза (ж) | [mómina səlzá] |
| snowdrop | кокиче (с) | [kokítʃe] |

nettle	коприва (ж)	[kopríva]
sorrel	киселец (м)	[kíselets]
water lily	водна лилия (ж)	[vódna lílija]
fern	папрат (м)	[páprat]
lichen	лишей (м)	[líʃej]

conservatory (greenhouse)	оранжерия (ж)	[oranʒérija]
lawn	тревна площ (ж)	[trévna ploʃt]
flowerbed	цветна леха (ж)	[tsvétna lehá]

plant	растение (с)	[rasténie]
grass	трева (ж)	[trevá]
blade of grass	тревичка (ж)	[trevítʃka]

leaf	лист (м)	[list]
petal	венчелистче (с)	[ventʃelísttʃe]
stem	стъбло (с)	[stəbló]
tuber	грудка (ж)	[grútka]

| young plant (shoot) | кълн (м) | [kəln] |
| thorn | бодил (м) | [bodíl] |

to blossom (vi)	цъфтя	[tsəftʲá]
to fade, to wither	увяхвам	[uvʲáhvam]
smell (odor)	мирис (м)	[míris]
to cut (flowers)	отрежа	[otréʒa]
to pick (a flower)	откъсна	[otkésna]

98. Cereals, grains

grain	зърно (с)	[zérno]
cereal crops	житни култури (ж мн)	[ʒítni kultúri]
ear (of barley, etc.)	клас (м)	[klas]

wheat	пшеница (ж)	[pʃenítsa]
rye	ръж (ж)	[rəʒ]
oats	овес (м)	[ovés]
millet	просо (с)	[prosó]
barley	ечемик (м)	[etʃemík]

corn	царевица (ж)	[tsárevitsa]
rice	ориз (м)	[oríz]
buckwheat	елда (ж)	[élda]

pea plant	грах (м)	[grah]
kidney bean	фасул (м)	[fasúl]
soy	соя (ж)	[sója]

lentil	**леща** (ж)	[léʃta]
beans (pulse crops)	**боб** (м)	[bop]

T&P BOOKS

COUNTRIES OF THE WORLD

T&P Books Publishing

Afghanistan	Афганистан	[afganistán]
Albania	Албания	[albánija]
Argentina	Аржентина	[arʒentína]
Armenia	Армения	[arménija]
Australia	Австралия	[afstrálija]
Austria	Австрия	[áfstrija]
Azerbaijan	Азербайджан	[azerbajdʒán]
The Bahamas	Бахамски острови	[bahámski óstrovi]
Bangladesh	Бангладеш	[bangladéʃ]
Belarus	Беларус	[belarús]
Belgium	Белгия	[bélgija]
Bolivia	Боливия	[bolívija]
Bosnia and Herzegovina	Босна и Херцеговина	[bósna i hertsegóvina]
Brazil	Бразилия	[brazílija]
Bulgaria	България	[bəlgárija]
Cambodia	Камбоджа	[kambódʒa]
Canada	Канада	[kanáda]
Chile	Чили	[ʧíli]
China	Китай	[kitáj]
Colombia	Колумбия	[kolúmbija]
Croatia	Хърватия	[hərvátija]
Cuba	Куба	[kúba]
Cyprus	Кипър	[kípər]
Czech Republic	Чехия	[ʧéhija]
Denmark	Дания	[dánija]
Dominican Republic	Доминиканска република	[dominikánska repúblika]
Ecuador	Еквадор	[ekvadór]
Egypt	Египет	[egípet]
England	Англия	[ánglija]
Estonia	Естония	[estónija]
Finland	Финландия	[finlándija]
France	Франция	[frántsija]
French Polynesia	Френска Полинезия	[frénska polinézija]
Georgia	Грузия	[grúzija]
Germany	Германия	[germánija]
Ghana	Гана	[gána]
Great Britain	Великобритания	[velikobritánija]
Greece	Гърция	[gə́rtsija]
Haiti	Хаити	[haíti]
Hungary	Унгария	[ungárija]

100. Countries. Part 2

Iceland	Исландия	[islándija]
India	Индия	[índija]
Indonesia	Индонезия	[indonézija]
Iran	Иран	[irán]
Iraq	Ирак	[irák]
Ireland	Ирландия	[irlándija]
Israel	Израел	[izráel]
Italy	Италия	[itálija]

Jamaica	Ямайка	[jamájka]
Japan	Япония	[japónija]
Jordan	Йордания	[jordánija]
Kazakhstan	Казахстан	[kazahstán]
Kenya	Кения	[kénija]
Kirghizia	Киргизстан	[kirgistán]
Kuwait	Кувейт	[kuvéjt]
Laos	Лаос	[laós]
Latvia	Латвия	[látvija]
Lebanon	Ливан	[liván]
Libya	Либия	[líbija]
Liechtenstein	Лихтенщайн	[líhtenʃtajn]
Lithuania	Литва	[lítva]
Luxembourg	Люксембург	[lʲúksemburg]

Macedonia (Republic of ~)	Македония	[makedónija]
Madagascar	Мадагаскар	[madagaskár]
Malaysia	Малайзия	[malájzija]
Malta	Малта	[málta]
Mexico	Мексико	[méksiko]
Moldova, Moldavia	Молдова	[moldóva]
Monaco	Монако	[monáko]
Mongolia	Монголия	[mongólija]
Montenegro	Черна гора	[tʲérna gorá]
Morocco	Мароко	[maróko]
Myanmar	Мянма	[mʲánma]
Namibia	Намибия	[namíbija]
Nepal	Непал	[nepál]
Netherlands	Нидерландия	[niderlándija]
New Zealand	Нова Зеландия	[nóva zelándija]
North Korea	Северна Корея	[séverna koréja]
Norway	Норвегия	[norvégija]

101. Countries. Part 3

Pakistan	Пакистан	[pakistán]
Palestine	Палестинска автономия	[palestínska aftonómija]

Panama	Панама	[panáma]
Paraguay	Парагвай	[paragváj]
Peru	Перу	[perú]
Poland	Полша	[pólʃa]
Portugal	Португалия	[portugálija]
Romania	Румъния	[ruménija]
Russia	Русия	[rusíja]
Saudi Arabia	Саудитска Арабия	[saudítska arábija]
Scotland	Шотландия	[ʃotlándija]
Senegal	Сенегал	[senegál]
Serbia	Сърбия	[sérbija]
Slovakia	Словакия	[slovákija]
Slovenia	Словения	[slovénija]
South Africa	Южноафриканска република	[juʒno·afrikánska repúblika]
South Korea	Южна Корея	[júʒna koréja]
Spain	Испания	[ispánija]
Suriname	Суринам	[surinám]
Sweden	Швеция	[ʃvétsija]
Switzerland	Швейцария	[ʃvejtsárija]
Syria	Сирия	[sírija]
Taiwan	Тайван	[tajván]
Tajikistan	Таджикистан	[tadʒikistán]
Tanzania	Танзания	[tanzánija]
Tasmania	Тасмания	[tasmánija]
Thailand	Тайланд	[tajlánt]
Tunisia	Тунис	[túnis]
Turkey	Турция	[túrtsija]
Turkmenistan	Туркменистан	[turkmenistán]
Ukraine	Украйна	[ukrájna]
United Arab Emirates	Обединени арабски емирства	[obedinéni arápski emírstva]
United States of America	Съединени американски щати	[sɤedinéni amerikánski ʃtáti]
Uruguay	Уругвай	[urugváj]
Uzbekistan	Узбекистан	[uzbekistán]
Vatican	Ватикана	[vatikána]
Venezuela	Венецуела	[venetsuéla]
Vietnam	Виетнам	[vietnám]
Zanzibar	Занзибар	[zanzibár]

GASTRONOMIC GLOSSARY

This section contains a lot of
words and terms associated
with food. This dictionary will
make it easier for you to
understand the menu at a
restaurant and choose
the right dish

T&P Books Publishing

English-Bulgarian gastronomic glossary

aftertaste	привкус (м)	[prífkus]
almond	бадем (м)	[badém]
anise	анасон (м)	[anasón]
aperitif	аперитив (м)	[aperitív]
appetite	апетит (м)	[apetít]
appetizer	мезе (с)	[mezé]
apple	ябълка (ж)	[jábəlka]
apricot	кайсия (ж)	[kajsíja]
artichoke	ангинар (м)	[anginár]
asparagus	аспержа (ж)	[aspérʒa]
Atlantic salmon	сьомга (ж)	[sʲómga]
avocado	авокадо (с)	[avokádo]
bacon	бекон (м)	[bekón]
banana	банан (м)	[banán]
barley	ечемик (м)	[etʃemík]
bartender	бармаn (м)	[bárman]
basil	босилек (м)	[bosílek]
bay leaf	дафинов лист (м)	[dafínov list]
beans	боб (м)	[bop]
beef	говеждо (с)	[govéʒdo]
beer	бира (ж)	[bíra]
beet	цвекло (с)	[tsveklό]
bell pepper	пипер (м)	[pipér]
berries	горски плодове (м мн)	[górski plodové]
berry	горски плод (м)	[górski plot]
bilberry	боровинки (ж мн)	[borovínki]
birch bolete	брезова манатарка (ж)	[brézova manatárka]
bitter	горчив	[gortʃív]
black coffee	черно кафе (с)	[tʃérno kafé]
black pepper	черен пипер (м)	[tʃéren pipér]
black tea	черен чай (м)	[tʃéren tʃaj]
blackberry	къпина (ж)	[kəpína]
blackcurrant	черно френско грозде (с)	[tʃérno frénsko grόzde]
boiled	варен	[varén]
bottle opener	отварачка (ж)	[otvarátʃka]
bread	хляб (м)	[hlʲap]
breakfast	закуска (ж)	[zakúska]
bream	платика (ж)	[platíka]
broccoli	броколи (с)	[brόkoli]
Brussels sprouts	брюкселско зеле (с)	[brʲúkselsko zéle]
buckwheat	елда (ж)	[élda]
butter	краве масло (с)	[kráve maslό]
buttercream	крем (м)	[krem]

cabbage	зеле (c)	[zéle]
cake	паста (ж)	[pásta]
cake	торта (ж)	[tórta]
calorie	калория (ж)	[kalórija]
can opener	отварачка (ж)	[otvarátʃka]
candy	бонбон (м)	[bonbón]
canned food	консерви (ж мн)	[konsérvi]
cappuccino	кафе (c) със сметана	[kafé səs smetána]
caraway	черен тмин (м)	[tʃéren tmin]
carbohydrates	въглехидрати (м мн)	[vəglehidráti]
carbonated	газирана	[gazíran]
carp	шаран (м)	[ʃarán]
carrot	морков (м)	[mórkof]
catfish	сом (м)	[som]
cauliflower	карфиол (м)	[karfiól]
caviar	хайвер (м)	[hajvér]
celery	целина (ж)	[tsélina]
cep	манатарка (ж)	[manatárka]
cereal crops	житни култури (ж мн)	[ʒítni kultúri]
champagne	шампанско (c)	[ʃampánsko]
chanterelle	пачи крак (м)	[pátʃi krak]
check	сметка (ж)	[smétka]
cheese	кашкавал (м)	[kaʃkavál]
chewing gum	дъвка (ж)	[dəfka]
chicken	кокошка (ж)	[kokóʃka]
chocolate	шоколад (м)	[ʃokolát]
chocolate	шоколадов	[ʃokoládov]
cinnamon	канела (ж)	[kanéla]
clear soup	бульон (м)	[buljón]
cloves	карамфил (м)	[karamfíl]
cocktail	коктейл (м)	[koktéjl]
coconut	кокосов орех (м)	[kokósov óreh]
cod	треска (ж)	[tréska]
coffee	кафе (c)	[kafé]
coffee with milk	кафе (c) с мляко	[kafé s mlʲáko]
cognac	коняк (м)	[konʲák]
cold	студен	[studén]
condensed milk	сгъстено мляко (c)	[sgəsténo mlʲáko]
condiment	подправка (ж)	[podpráfka]
confectionery	сладкарски изделия (c мн)	[slatkárski izdélija]
cookies	бисквити (ж мн)	[biskvíti]
coriander	кориандър (м)	[koriándər]
corkscrew	тирбушон (м)	[tirbuʃón]
corn	царевица (ж)	[tsárevitsa]
corn	царевица (ж)	[tsárevitsa]
cornflakes	царевичен флейкс (м)	[tsárevitʃen flejks]
course, dish	ястие (c)	[jástie]
cowberry	червена боровинка (ж)	[tʃervéna borovínka]
crab	морски рак (м)	[mórski rak]
cranberry	клюква (ж)	[klʲúkva]
cream	каймак (м)	[kajmák]

crumb	троха (ж)	[trohá]
cucumber	краставица (ж)	[krástavitsa]
cuisine	кухня (ж)	[kúhnⁱa]
cup	чаша (ж)	[ʧáʃa]
dark beer	тъмна бира (ж)	[témna bíra]
date	фурма (ж)	[furmá]
death cap	зелена мухоморка (ж)	[zeléna muhómorka]
dessert	десерт (м)	[desért]
diet	диета (ж)	[diéta]
dill	копър (м)	[kópər]
dinner	вечеря (ж)	[veʧérⁱa]
dried	сушен	[suʃén]
drinking water	питейна вода (ж)	[pitéjna vodá]
duck	патица (ж)	[pátitsa]
ear	клас (м)	[klas]
edible mushroom	ядлива гъба (ж)	[jadlíva géba]
eel	змиорка (ж)	[zmiórka]
egg	яйце (с)	[jajtsé]
egg white	белтък (м)	[bɛlték]
egg yolk	жълтък (м)	[ʒəlték]
eggplant	патладжан (м)	[patladʒán]
eggs	яйца (с мн)	[jajtsá]
Enjoy your meal!	Добър апетит!	[dobér apetít]
fats	мазнини (ж мн)	[maznіní]
fig	смокиня (ж)	[smokínⁱa]
filling	плънка (ж)	[plénka]
fish	риба (ж)	[ríba]
flatfish	калкан (м)	[kalkán]
flour	брашно (с)	[braʃnó]
fly agaric	мухоморка (ж)	[muhomórka]
food	храна (ж)	[hraná]
fork	вилица (ж)	[vílitsa]
freshly squeezed juice	фреш (м)	[freʃ]
fried	пържен	[pérʒen]
fried eggs	пържени яйца (с мн)	[pérʒeni jajtsá]
frozen	замразен	[zamrazén]
fruit	плод (м)	[plot]
fruits	плодове (м мн)	[plodové]
game	дивеч (ж)	[díveʧ]
gammon	бут (м)	[but]
garlic	чесън (м)	[ʧésən]
gin	джин (м)	[dʒin]
ginger	джинджифил (м)	[dʒindʒifíl]
glass	стакан (м)	[stakán]
glass	чаша (ж) за вино	[ʧáʃa za víno]
goose	гъска (ж)	[géska]
gooseberry	цариградско грозде (с)	[tsarigrátsko grózde]
grain	зърно (с)	[zérno]
grape	грозде (с)	[grózde]
grapefruit	грейпфрут (м)	[gréjpfrut]
green tea	зелен чай (м)	[zelén ʧaj]
greens	зарзават (м)	[zarzavát]

groats	грис, булгур (м)	[gris], [bulgúr]
halibut	палтус (м)	[páltus]
ham	шунка (ж)	[ʃúnka]
hamburger	кайма (ж)	[kajmá]
hamburger	хамбургер (м)	[hámburger]
hazelnut	лешник (м)	[léʃnik]
herring	селда (ж)	[sélda]
honey	мед (м)	[met]
horseradish	хрян (м)	[hrʲan]
hot	горещ	[goréʃt]
ice	лед (м)	[let]
ice-cream	сладолед (м)	[sladolét]
instant coffee	разтворимо кафе (с)	[rastvorímo kafé]
jam	конфитюр (м)	[konfitʲúr]
jam	сладко (с)	[slátko]
juice	сок (м)	[sok]
kidney bean	фасул (м)	[fasúl]
kiwi	киви (с)	[kívi]
knife	нож (м)	[noʒ]
lamb	агнешко (с)	[ágneʃko]
lemon	лимон (м)	[limón]
lemonade	лимонада (ж)	[limonáda]
lentil	леща (ж)	[léʃta]
lettuce	салата (ж)	[saláta]
light beer	светла бира (ж)	[svétla bíra]
liqueur	ликьор (м)	[likʲór]
liquors	спиртни напитки (ж мн)	[spírtni napítki]
liver	черен дроб (м)	[tʃéren drop]
lunch	обяд (м)	[obʲát]
mackerel	скумрия (ж)	[skumríja]
mandarin	мандарина (ж)	[mandarína]
mango	манго (с)	[mángo]
margarine	маргарин (м)	[margarín]
marmalade	мармалад (м)	[marmalát]
mashed potatoes	картофено пюре (с)	[kartófeno pʲuré]
mayonnaise	майонеза (ж)	[majonéza]
meat	месо (с)	[mesó]
melon	пъпеш (м)	[pə́peʃ]
menu	меню (с)	[menʲú]
milk	мляко (с)	[mlʲáko]
milkshake	млечен коктейл (м)	[mlétʃen koktéjl]
millet	просо (с)	[prosó]
mineral water	минерална вода (ж)	[minerálna vodá]
morel	пумпалка (ж)	[púmpalka]
mushroom	гъба (ж)	[gə́ba]
mustard	горчица (ж)	[gortʃítsa]
non-alcoholic	безалкохолен	[bezalkohólen]
noodles	юфка (ж)	[jufká]
oats	овес (м)	[ovés]
olive oil	зехтин (м)	[zehtín]
olives	маслини (ж мн)	[maslíni]
omelet	омлет (м)	[omlét]

onion	лук (м)	[luk]
orange	портокал (м)	[portokál]
orange juice	портокалов сок (м)	[portokálov sok]
orange-cap boletus	червена брезовка (ж)	[tʃervéna brézofka]
oyster	стрида (ж)	[strída]
pâté	пастет (м)	[pastét]
papaya	папая (ж)	[papája]
paprika	червен пипер (м)	[tʃervén pipér]
parsley	магданоз (м)	[magdanóz]
pasta	макарони (мн)	[makaróni]
pea	грах (м)	[grah]
peach	праскова (ж)	[práskova]
peanut	фъстък (м)	[fəsték]
pear	круша (ж)	[krúʃa]
peel	кожа (ж)	[kóʒa]
perch	костур (м)	[kostúr]
pickled	маринован	[marinóvan]
pie	пирог (м)	[pirók]
piece	парче (с)	[partʃé]
pike	щука (ж)	[ʃtúka]
pike perch	бяла риба (ж)	[bʲála ríba]
pineapple	ананас (м)	[ananás]
pistachios	шамфъстъци (м мн)	[ʃamfəstétsi]
pizza	пица (ж)	[pítsa]
plate	чиния (ж)	[tʃiníja]
plum	слива (ж)	[slíva]
poisonous mushroom	отровна гъба (ж)	[otróvna gə́ba]
pomegranate	нар (м)	[nar]
pork	свинско (с)	[svínsko]
porridge	каша (ж)	[káʃa]
portion	порция (ж)	[pórtsija]
potato	картофи (мн)	[kartófi]
proteins	белтъчини (ж мн)	[beltətʃiní]
pub, bar	бар (м)	[bar]
pumpkin	тиква (ж)	[tíkva]
rabbit	питомен заек (м)	[pítomen záek]
radish	репичка (ж)	[répitʃka]
raisin	стафиди (ж мн)	[stafídi]
raspberry	малина (ж)	[malína]
recipe	рецепта (ж)	[retsépta]
red pepper	червен пипер (м)	[tʃervén pipér]
red wine	червено вино (с)	[tʃervéno víno]
redcurrant	червено френско грозде (с)	[tʃervéno frénsko grózde]
refreshing drink	разхладителна напитка (ж)	[rashladítelna napítka]
rice	ориз (м)	[oríz]
rum	ром (м)	[rom]
russula	гълъбка (ж)	[gə́ləpka]
rye	ръж (ж)	[rəʒ]
saffron	шафран (м)	[ʃafrán]
salad	салата (ж)	[saláta]

salmon	сьомга (ж)	[sʲómga]
salt	сол (ж)	[sol]
salty	солен	[solén]
sandwich	сандвич (м)	[sándvitʃ]
sardine	сардина (ж)	[sardína]
sauce	сос (м)	[sos]
saucer	чинийка (ж)	[tʃiníjka]
sausage	салам (м)	[salám]
seafood	морски продукти (м мн)	[mórski prodúkti]
sesame	сусам (м)	[susám]
shark	акула (ж)	[akúla]
shrimp	скарида (ж)	[skarída]
side dish	гарнитура (ж)	[garnitúra]
slice	резенче (с)	[rézentʃe]
smoked	пушен	[púʃen]
soft drink	безалкохолна напитка (ж)	[bezalkohólna napítka]
soup	супа (ж)	[súpa]
soup spoon	супена лъжица (ж)	[súpena ləʒítsa]
sour cherry	вишна (ж)	[víʃna]
sour cream	сметана (ж)	[smetána]
soy	соя (ж)	[sója]
spaghetti	спагети (мн)	[spagéti]
sparkling	газирана	[gazíran]
spice	подправка (ж)	[podpráfka]
spinach	спанак (м)	[spanák]
spiny lobster	лангуста (ж)	[langústa]
spoon	лъжица (ж)	[ləʒítsa]
squid	калмар (м)	[kalmár]
steak	бифтек (м)	[bifték]
still	негазирана	[negazíran]
strawberry	ягода (ж)	[jágoda]
sturgeon	есетра (ж)	[esétra]
sugar	захар (ж)	[záhar]
sunflower oil	слънчогледово масло (с)	[sləntʃoglédovo máslo]
sweet	сладък	[sládək]
sweet cherry	череша (ж)	[tʃeréʃa]
taste, flavor	вкус (м)	[fkus]
tasty	вкусен	[fkúsen]
tea	чай (м)	[tʃaj]
teaspoon	чаена лъжица (ж)	[tʃáena ləʒítsa]
tip	бакшиш (м)	[bakʃíʃ]
tomato	домат (м)	[domát]
tomato juice	доматен сок (м)	[domáten sok]
tongue	език (м)	[ezík]
toothpick	клечка (ж) за зъби	[klétʃka za zébi]
trout	пъстърва (ж)	[pəstérva]
tuna	риба тон (м)	[ríba ton]
turkey	пуйка (ж)	[pújka]
turnip	ряпа (ж)	[rʲápa]
veal	телешко месо (с)	[téleʃko mesó]

vegetable oil	**олио** (с)	[ólio]
vegetables	**зеленчуци** (м мн)	[zelentʃútsi]
vegetarian	**вегетарианец** (м)	[vegetariánets]
vegetarian	**вегетариански**	[vegetariánski]
vermouth	**вермут** (м)	[vermút]
vienna sausage	**кренвирш** (м)	[krénvirʃ]
vinegar	**оцет** (м)	[otsét]
vitamin	**витамин** (м)	[vitamín]
vodka	**водка** (ж)	[vótka]
wafers	**вафли** (ж мн)	[váfli]
waiter	**сервитьор** (м)	[servitʲór]
waitress	**сервитьорка** (ж)	[servitʲórka]
walnut	**орех** (м)	[óreh]
water	**вода** (ж)	[vodá]
watermelon	**диня** (ж)	[dínʲa]
wheat	**пшеница** (ж)	[pʃenítsa]
whiskey	**уиски** (с)	[wíski]
white wine	**бяло вино** (с)	[bʲálo víno]
wild strawberry	**горска ягода** (ж)	[górska jágoda]
wine	**вино** (с)	[víno]
wine list	**карта** (ж) **на виното**	[kárta na vínoto]
with ice	**с лед**	[s let]
yogurt	**йогурт** (м)	[jógurt]
zucchini	**тиквичка** (ж)	[tíkvitʃka]

Bulgarian-English gastronomic glossary

авокадо (с)	[avokádo]	avocado
агнешко (с)	[ágneʃko]	lamb
акула (ж)	[akúla]	shark
ананас (м)	[ananás]	pineapple
анасон (м)	[anasón]	anise
ангинар (м)	[anginár]	artichoke
аперитив (м)	[aperitív]	aperitif
апетит (м)	[apetít]	appetite
аспержа (ж)	[aspérʒa]	asparagus
бадем (м)	[badém]	almond
бакшиш (м)	[bakʃíʃ]	tip
банан (м)	[banán]	banana
бар (м)	[bar]	pub, bar
барман (м)	[bárman]	bartender
безалкохолен	[bezalkohólen]	non-alcoholic
безалкохолна напитка (ж)	[bezalkohólna napítka]	soft drink
бекон (м)	[bekón]	bacon
белтък (м)	[belték]	egg white
белтъчини (ж мн)	[beltətʃíní]	proteins
бира (ж)	[bíra]	beer
бисквити (ж мн)	[biskvíti]	cookies
бифтек (м)	[bifték]	steak
боб (м)	[bop]	beans
бонбон (м)	[bonbón]	candy
боровинки (ж мн)	[borovínki]	bilberry
босилек (м)	[bosílek]	basil
брашно (с)	[braʃnó]	flour
брезова манатарка (ж)	[brézova manatárka]	birch bolete
броколи (ж)	[brókoli]	broccoli
брюкселско зеле (с)	[brʲúkselsko zéle]	Brussels sprouts
бульон (м)	[buljón]	clear soup
бут (м)	[but]	gammon
бяла риба (ж)	[bʲála ríba]	pike perch
бяло вино (с)	[bʲálo víno]	white wine
варен	[varén]	boiled
вафли (ж мн)	[váfli]	wafers
вегетарианец (м)	[vegetariánets]	vegetarian
вегетариански	[vegetariánski]	vegetarian
вермут (м)	[vermút]	vermouth
вечеря (ж)	[vetʃérʲa]	dinner
вилица (ж)	[vílitsa]	fork
вино (с)	[víno]	wine
витамин (м)	[vitamín]	vitamin

вишна (ж)	[víʃna]	sour cherry
вкус (м)	[fkus]	taste, flavor
вкусен	[fkúsen]	tasty
вода (ж)	[vodá]	water
водка (ж)	[vótka]	vodka
въглехидрати (м мн)	[vəglehidráti]	carbohydrates
газирана	[gazíran]	carbonated
газирана	[gazíran]	sparkling
гарнитура (ж)	[garnitúra]	side dish
говеждо (с)	[govéʒdo]	beef
горещ	[goréʃt]	hot
горска ягода (ж)	[górska jágoda]	wild strawberry
горски плод (м)	[górski plot]	berry
горски плодове (м мн)	[górski plodové]	berries
горчив	[gortʃív]	bitter
горчица (ж)	[gortʃítsa]	mustard
грах (м)	[grah]	pea
грейпфрут (м)	[gréjpfrut]	grapefruit
грис, булгур (м)	[gris], [bulgúr]	groats
грозде (с)	[grózde]	grape
гъба (ж)	[gəba]	mushroom
гълъбка (ж)	[gə́ləpka]	russula
гъска (ж)	[gə́ska]	goose
дафинов лист (м)	[dafínov list]	bay leaf
десерт (м)	[desért]	dessert
джин (м)	[dʒin]	gin
джинджифил (м)	[dʒindʒifíl]	ginger
дивеч (ж)	[dívetʃ]	game
диета (ж)	[diéta]	diet
диня (ж)	[dínʲa]	watermelon
Добър апетит!	[dobér apetít]	Enjoy your meal!
домат (м)	[domát]	tomato
доматен сок (м)	[domáten sok]	tomato juice
дъвка (ж)	[də́fka]	chewing gum
език (м)	[ezík]	tongue
елда (ж)	[élda]	buckwheat
есетра (ж)	[esétra]	sturgeon
ечемик (м)	[etʃemík]	barley
житни култури (ж мн)	[ʒítni kultúri]	cereal crops
жълтък (м)	[ʒəltə́k]	egg yolk
закуска (ж)	[zakúska]	breakfast
замразен	[zamrazén]	frozen
зарзават (м)	[zarzavát]	greens
захар (ж)	[záhar]	sugar
зеле (с)	[zéle]	cabbage
зелен чай (м)	[zelén tʃaj]	green tea
зелена мухоморка (ж)	[zeléna muhómorka]	death cap
зеленчуци (м мн)	[zelentʃútsi]	vegetables
зехтин (м)	[zehtín]	olive oil
змиорка (ж)	[zmiórka]	eel
зърно (с)	[zérno]	grain
йогурт (м)	[jógurt]	yogurt

кайма (ж)	[kajmá]	hamburger
каймак (м)	[kajmák]	cream
кайсия (ж)	[kajsíja]	apricot
калкан (м)	[kalkán]	flatfish
калмар (м)	[kalmár]	squid
калория (ж)	[kalórija]	calorie
канела (ж)	[kanéla]	cinnamon
карамфил (м)	[karamfíl]	cloves
карта (ж) на виното	[kárta na vínoto]	wine list
картофено пюре (с)	[kartófeno pʲuré]	mashed potatoes
картофи (мн)	[kartófi]	potato
карфиол (м)	[karfiól]	cauliflower
кафе (с)	[kafé]	coffee
кафе (с) с мляко	[kafé s mlʲáko]	coffee with milk
кафе (с) със сметана	[kafé səs smetána]	cappuccino
каша (ж)	[káʃa]	porridge
кашкавал (м)	[kaʃkavál]	cheese
киви (с)	[kívi]	kiwi
клас (м)	[klas]	ear
клечка (ж) за зъби	[kléʧka za zébi]	toothpick
клюква (ж)	[klʲúkva]	cranberry
кожа (ж)	[kóʒa]	peel
кокосов орех (м)	[kokósov óreh]	coconut
кокошка (ж)	[kokóʃka]	chicken
коктейл (м)	[koktéjl]	cocktail
консерви (ж мн)	[konsérvi]	canned food
конфитюр (м)	[konfitʲúr]	jam
коняк (м)	[konʲák]	cognac
копър (м)	[kópər]	dill
кориандър (м)	[koriándər]	coriander
костур (м)	[kostúr]	perch
краве масло (с)	[kráve masló]	butter
краставица (ж)	[krástavitsa]	cucumber
крем (м)	[krem]	buttercream
кренвирш (м)	[krénvirʃ]	vienna sausage
круша (ж)	[krúʃa]	pear
кухня (ж)	[kúhnʲa]	cuisine
къпина (ж)	[kəpína]	blackberry
лангуста (ж)	[langústa]	spiny lobster
лед (м)	[let]	ice
лешник (м)	[léʃnik]	hazelnut
леща (ж)	[léʃta]	lentil
ликьор (м)	[likʲór]	liqueur
лимон (м)	[limón]	lemon
лимонада (ж)	[limonáda]	lemonade
лук (м)	[luk]	onion
лъжица (ж)	[ləʒítsa]	spoon
магданоз (м)	[magdanóz]	parsley
мазнини (ж мн)	[mazniní]	fats
майонеза (ж)	[majonéza]	mayonnaise
макарони (мн)	[makaróni]	pasta
малина (ж)	[malína]	raspberry

манатарка (ж)	[manatárka]	cep
манго (с)	[mángo]	mango
мандарина (ж)	[mandarína]	mandarin
маргарин (м)	[margarín]	margarine
маринован	[marinóvan]	pickled
мармалад (м)	[marmalát]	marmalade
маслини (ж мн)	[maslíni]	olives
мед (м)	[met]	honey
мезе (с)	[mezé]	appetizer
меню (с)	[menʲú]	menu
месо (с)	[mesó]	meat
минерална вода (ж)	[minerálna vodá]	mineral water
млечен коктейл (м)	[mlétʃen koktéjl]	milkshake
мляко (с)	[mlʲáko]	milk
морков (м)	[mórkof]	carrot
морски продукти (м мн)	[mórski prodúkti]	seafood
морски рак (м)	[mórski rak]	crab
мухоморка (ж)	[muhomórka]	fly agaric
нар (м)	[nar]	pomegranate
негазирана	[negazíran]	still
нож (м)	[noʒ]	knife
обяд (м)	[obʲát]	lunch
овес (м)	[ovés]	oats
олио (с)	[ólio]	vegetable oil
омлет (м)	[omlét]	omelet
орех (м)	[óreh]	walnut
ориз (м)	[oríz]	rice
отварачка (ж)	[otvarátʃka]	bottle opener
отварачка (ж)	[otvarátʃka]	can opener
отровна гъба (ж)	[otróvna géba]	poisonous mushroom
оцет (м)	[otsét]	vinegar
палтус (м)	[páltus]	halibut
папая (ж)	[papája]	papaya
парче (с)	[partʃé]	piece
паста (ж)	[pásta]	cake
пастет (м)	[pastét]	pâté
патица (ж)	[pátitsa]	duck
патладжан (м)	[patladʒán]	eggplant
пачи крак (м)	[pátʃi krak]	chanterelle
пипер (м)	[pipér]	bell pepper
пирог (м)	[pirók]	pie
питейна вода (ж)	[pitéjna vodá]	drinking water
питомен заек (м)	[pítomen záek]	rabbit
пица (ж)	[pítsa]	pizza
платика (ж)	[platíka]	bream
плод (м)	[plot]	fruit
плодове (м мн)	[plodové]	fruits
плънка (ж)	[plénka]	filling
подправка (ж)	[podpráfka]	condiment
подправка (ж)	[podpráfka]	spice
портокал (м)	[portokál]	orange
портокалов сок (м)	[portokálov sok]	orange juice

порция (ж)	[pórtsija]	portion
праскова (ж)	[práskova]	peach
привкус (м)	[prífkus]	aftertaste
просо (с)	[prosó]	millet
пуйка (ж)	[pújka]	turkey
пумпалка (ж)	[púmpalka]	morel
пушен	[púʃen]	smoked
пшеница (ж)	[pʃenítsa]	wheat
пъпеш (м)	[pépeʃ]	melon
пържен	[pérʒen]	fried
пържени яйца (с мн)	[pérʒeni jajtsá]	fried eggs
пъстърва (ж)	[pəstérva]	trout
разтворимо кафе (с)	[rastvorímo kafé]	instant coffee
разхладителна напитка (ж)	[rashladítelna napítka]	refreshing drink
резенче (с)	[rézentʃe]	slice
репичка (ж)	[répitʃka]	radish
рецепта (ж)	[retsépta]	recipe
риба (ж)	[ríba]	fish
риба тон (м)	[ríba ton]	tuna
ром (м)	[rom]	rum
ръж (ж)	[rəʒ]	rye
ряпа (ж)	[rʲápa]	turnip
с лед	[s let]	with ice
салам (м)	[salám]	sausage
салата (ж)	[saláta]	lettuce
салата (ж)	[saláta]	salad
сандвич (м)	[sándvitʃ]	sandwich
сардина (ж)	[sardína]	sardine
светла бира (ж)	[svétla bíra]	light beer
свинско (с)	[svínsko]	pork
сгъстено мляко (с)	[sgəsténo mlʲáko]	condensed milk
селда (ж)	[sélda]	herring
сервитьор (м)	[servitʲór]	waiter
сервитьорка (ж)	[servitʲórka]	waitress
скарида (ж)	[skarída]	shrimp
скумрия (ж)	[skumríja]	mackerel
сладкарски изделия (с мн)	[slatkárski izdélija]	confectionery
сладко (с)	[slátko]	jam
сладолед (м)	[sladolét]	ice-cream
сладък	[sládək]	sweet
слива (ж)	[slíva]	plum
слънчогледово масло (с)	[sləntʃoglédovo máslo]	sunflower oil
сметана (ж)	[smetána]	sour cream
сметка (ж)	[smétka]	check
смокиня (ж)	[smokínʲa]	fig
сок (м)	[sok]	juice
сол (ж)	[sol]	salt
солен	[solén]	salty
сом (м)	[som]	catfish

сос (м)	[sos]	sauce
соя (ж)	[sója]	soy
спагети (мн)	[spagéti]	spaghetti
спанак (м)	[spanák]	spinach
спиртни напитки (ж мн)	[spírtni napítki]	liquors
стакан (м)	[stakán]	glass
стафиди (ж мн)	[stafídi]	raisin
стрида (ж)	[strída]	oyster
студен	[studén]	cold
супа (ж)	[súpa]	soup
супена лъжица (ж)	[súpena ləʒítsa]	soup spoon
сусам (м)	[susám]	sesame
сушен	[suʃén]	dried
сьомга (ж)	[sʲómga]	salmon
сьомга (ж)	[sʲómga]	Atlantic salmon
телешко месо (с)	[téleʃko mesó]	veal
тиква (ж)	[tíkva]	pumpkin
тиквичка (ж)	[tíkviʧka]	zucchini
тирбушон (м)	[tirbuʃón]	corkscrew
торта (ж)	[tórta]	cake
треска (ж)	[tréska]	cod
троха (ж)	[trohá]	crumb
тъмна бира (ж)	[təmna bíra]	dark beer
уиски (с)	[wíski]	whiskey
фасул (м)	[fasúl]	kidney bean
фреш (м)	[freʃ]	freshly squeezed juice
фурма (ж)	[furmá]	date
фъстък (м)	[fəstə́k]	peanut
хайвер (м)	[hajvér]	caviar
хамбургер (м)	[hámburger]	hamburger
хляб (м)	[hlʲap]	bread
храна (ж)	[hraná]	food
хрян (м)	[hrʲan]	horseradish
царевица (ж)	[tsárevitsa]	corn
царевица (ж)	[tsárevitsa]	corn
царевичен флейкс (м)	[tsárevitʃen flejks]	cornflakes
цариградско грозде (с)	[tsarigrátsko grózde]	gooseberry
цвекло (с)	[tsveklό]	beet
целина (ж)	[tsélina]	celery
чаена лъжица (ж)	[ʧáena ləʒítsa]	teaspoon
чай (м)	[ʧaj]	tea
чаша (ж)	[ʧáʃa]	cup
чаша (ж) за вино	[ʧáʃa za víno]	glass
червен пипер (м)	[ʧervén pipér]	red pepper
червен пипер (м)	[ʧervén pipér]	paprika
червена боровинка (ж)	[ʧervéna borovínka]	cowberry
червена брезовка (ж)	[ʧervéna brézofka]	orange-cap boletus
червено вино (с)	[ʧervéno víno]	red wine
червено френско грозде (с)	[ʧervéno frénsko grózde]	redcurrant
черен дроб (м)	[ʧéren drop]	liver
черен пипер (м)	[ʧéren pipér]	black pepper

черен тмин (м)	[tʃéren tmin]	caraway
черен чай (м)	[tʃéren tʃaj]	black tea
череша (ж)	[tʃeréʃa]	sweet cherry
черно кафе (с)	[tʃérno kafé]	black coffee
черно френско грозде (с)	[tʃérno frénsko grózde]	blackcurrant
чесън (м)	[tʃésən]	garlic
чинийка (ж)	[tʃiníjka]	saucer
чиния (ж)	[tʃiníja]	plate
шампанско (с)	[ʃampánsko]	champagne
шамфъстъци (м мн)	[ʃamfəstétsi]	pistachios
шаран (м)	[ʃarán]	carp
шафран (м)	[ʃafrán]	saffron
шоколад (м)	[ʃokolát]	chocolate
шоколадов	[ʃokoládov]	chocolate
шунка (ж)	[ʃúnka]	ham
щука (ж)	[ʃtúka]	pike
юфка (ж)	[jufká]	noodles
ябълка (ж)	[jábəlka]	apple
ягода (ж)	[jágoda]	strawberry
ядлива гъба (ж)	[jadlíva géba]	edible mushroom
яйца (с мн)	[jajtsá]	eggs
яйце (с)	[jajtsé]	egg
ястие (с)	[jástie]	course, dish